FAST AND ABSTINENCE IN THE FIRST ORDER OF SAINT FRANCIS

THE CATHOLIC UNIVERSITY OF AMERICA
CANON LAW STUDIES
No. 374

FAST AND ABSTINENCE IN THE FIRST ORDER OF SAINT FRANCIS

A HISTORICAL SYNOPSIS AND A COMMENTARY

A DISSERTATION

SUBMITTED TO THE FACULTY OF THE SCHOOL OF CANON LAW OF THE CATHOLIC UNIVERSITY OF AMERICA IN PARTIAL FULFILLMENT OF THE REQUIREMENTS FOR THE DEGREE OF DOCTOR OF CANON LAW

BY

REV. JORDAN JOSEPH SULLIVAN, O.F.M.CAP., B.A., J.C.L.
PRIEST OF THE NEW YORK PROVINCE OF SAINT MARY

THE CATHOLIC UNIVERSITY OF AMERICA PRESS
WASHINGTON, D. C.
1957

Nihil Obstat:
BERTRANDUS SCULLY, O.F.M.Cap., M.A.
Censor Deputatus

NATHANAEL SONNTAG, O.F.M.Cap., J.C.D.
Censor Deputatus

Praesentibus litteris permittimus ut dissertatio cui titulus: *FAST AND ABSTINENCE IN THE FIRST ORDER OF SAINT FRANCIS,* a R.P. Iordano a Yonkers Provinciae Nostrae Neo-Eboracensis alumno compositus et a duobus sacerdotibus revisus et probatus, servatis servandis, typis imprimatur et in lucem edatur.

Romae, in Curia Nostra Generali, die 5 martii 1957.

FR. BENIGNUS A SANT'ILARIO M.
Minister Generalis O.F.M.Cap.

Nihil Obstat:
ROMAEUS W. O'BRIEN, O. Carm., J.C.D.
Censor Deputatus

Imprimatur:
PATRICIUS A. O'BOYLE
Archiepiscopus Washingtoniensis

Washingtonii, die 25 februarii 1957.

PRINTED IN THE UNITED STATES OF AMERICA
9

Mariae
Reginae Ordinis Minorum

TABLE OF CONTENTS

CHAPTER II

CHAPTER III

FOREWORD

Inasmuch as it directly affects almost every professed member at some time in his life, the discipline of fast and abstinence in a religious Order is of general practical interest and importance. Frequently it is a discipline that is fraught with difficulties, when it becomes necessary to apply the dispositions of the religious Rule or of the Constitutions to varying concrete circumstances. The present work will treat of that discipline and of some of its difficulties as it exists in the First Order of Saint Francis.

The First Order of Saint Francis was founded in the early years of the thirteenth century. Almost from its very inception there were forces at work within the Order which later brought about its division. That division was first internal. Later it became external when, in the year 1517, Pope Leo X constituted two juridically distinct Franciscan families of the First Order:—the Order of Friars Minor of the Observance, and the Order of Friars Minor Conventual. In the year 1619, a third family was given its independent status. This family is the Order of Friars Minor Capuchin.

From the time of the first external division of the Order until the end of the nineteenth century, other internal divisions developed within the Order of Friars Minor of the Observance. In the year 1897, Pope Leo XIII united these several divisions into what is presently known as the Order of Friars Minor. Thus today the First Order of Saint Francis exists in three separate and independent branches:—the Order of Friars Minor, the Order of Friars Minor Conventual, and the Order of Friars Minor Capuchin.

Despite the various divisions that the Order has seen, past and present, every division has retained the same Rule as its fundamental body of laws. This dissertation will attempt, first of all, to explain the legislation that that Rule proposes on fasting. Then it will trace and explain the development of other legal dispositions that came into play in shaping the general discipline of fast and abstinence in the Order in its several branches.

A very important and a very interesting subordinate question that suggested itself to the writer during the preparation of this dissertation was the question relative to the binding character of Franciscan legislation on fast and abstinence. After due consideration, however, in view of the specific purpose of the dissertation, it was deemed best to omit all discussion of that question because of the difficulties and complexities which it presents.

For the sake of simplicity, the phrase *Franciscan Order* will be generally used throughout the dissertation in place of the more accurate yet cumbersome phrase *First Order of Saint Francis.* Similarly, to avoid confusion, the phrase *Order of Friars Minor* will ordinarily be used only in reference to that branch of the Order which Pope Leo XIII formed from a union of the various divisions within the Order of Friars Minor of the Observance. For a like reason, the present Rule, which is common to all three Franciscan families, will generally be referred to as the *Franciscan Rule,* and not as the *Rule of the Friars Minor.* Whenever an English excerpt of the Franciscan Rule appears in the text, the translation is that which was published by the American Capuchin Fathers of the Calvary Province in 1945.[1]

The writer wishes to take this occasion to express his profound thanks to all who have contributed toward making this dissertation possible. In the first place, that thanks is owed to his religious Superiors:—to the Very Reverend Adrian Holzmeister, O.F.M.Cap., past Minister Provincial of the Capuchin Province of Saint Mary; to the Very Reverend Seraphin Winterroth, O.F.M.Cap., present Minister Provincial of that same Province; and to the Reverend Firmin Schmidt, O.F.M.Cap., Guardian of Capuchin College, Washington, D. C. Secondly, he wishes to thank those who helped him in a more direct way in his study of Canon Law: —his former professors of Canon Law at Saint Anthony Friary, Marathon, Wisconsin; his professors at the Gregorian University,

[1] *Rule and Testament of the Seraphic Father Saint Francis and Constitutions of the Capuchin Friars Minor of Saint Francis* (Detroit: Province of St. Joseph of the Capuchin Order, 1945).

Rome, Italy; and his professors at the Catholic University of America, Washington, D. C. In a special way, he wishes to express his gratitude to the Very Reverend Sylvester Brielmaier, O.F.M.Cap., Librarian at the Capuchin International College of Saint Lawrence of Brindisi, Rome, Italy, who made available most of the material that served as a basis for this dissertation. Finally, he offers his sincere thanks to all those others who, in so many ways, have helped to bring this dissertation into its present final form.

FAST AND ABSTINENCE IN THE FIRST ORDER OF SAINT FRANCIS

ABBREVIATIONS

AAS—Acta Apostolicae Sedis
AFH—Archivum Franciscanum Historicum
AOFM—Acta Ordinis Fratrum Minorum
AOFMC—Analecta Ordinis Fratrum Minorum Capuccinorum
COFMC—Commentarium Ordinis Fratrum Minorum Conventualium
IS—Ius Seraphicum

CHAPTER I

THE LEGISLATION OF THE FRANCISCAN RULE

INTRODUCTION

The ten articles into which this first chapter is divided treat principally of the prescriptions laid down by the Rule of the First Order of Saint Francis on fast and abstinence. Actually, the discussion of the Rule begins only with the third article. In order to make the study reasonably complete, two introductory articles have been inserted. The first of these articles deals with the example set by Saint Francis. No adequate treatment of fast and abstinence in the Order could be undertaken without a study of his life. He is the model and the ideal of every Franciscan. His spirit is the spirit that gives purpose to the dead letter of the Franciscan law on fast and abstinence, and transforms it into a living act of love of God. The second article is primarily of historical interest. It deals with legislation in the Order on fast and abstinence previous to the approbation of the present Rule, the *Regula Bullata* of 1223.

ARTICLE I. THE FASTING OF SAINT FRANCIS

The spirit of fasting in the Franciscan Order extends far beyond the positive legislation found in the Rule. It finds its concretization in the life of Saint Francis, who was the living exemplar of the Franciscan ideal. The Rule demands comparatively little by way of fasting. Francis' life, on the other hand, was almost a continuous fast. It was an uninterrupted manifestation of his love for Christ.

To the two "Lents" commonly kept by the faithful of the time, the one preceding Christmas and the one preceding Easter,[1]

[1] Herrera, *Legislación Eclesiástica sobre el Ayuno y la Abstinencia,* Universidad Católica de América Estudios Canónicos, n. 92 (Washington, D.C.: The Catholic University of America, 1935), pp. 43–44; p. 61; C. 2, X, *de observatione ieiuniorum,* III, 46.

Francis added the observance of five voluntary "Lents": 1) that from Low Sunday until Pentecost; 2) that from Pentecost until the Feast of Saints Peter and Paul; 3) that from the Feast of Saints Peter and Paul until the Assumption; 4) that from the Assumption until the Feast of Saint Michael; and 5) that during the forty days following the Feast of the Epiphany.[2]

The length and the frequency of Saint Francis' fasts were most rigorous. The manner in which he fasted was no less rigorous. He took hardly enough nourishment to meet the requirements of nature, saying that it was a difficult thing to satisfy the needs of the body without making concessions to sensuality. When in good health, he hardly ever ate cooked food. If he did, he would first

[2] "Praerogativa quoque peculiaris devotionis ad ipsum ab Epiphaniae festo usque ad continuos quadraginta dies, eo scilicet tempore, quo Christus latuit in deserto, ad solitudinis loca declinans cellaque reclusus, quanta poterat arctitudine cibi et potus, ieiuniis, orationibus et laudibus Dei sine intermissione vacabat. . . . Matrem Domini Iesu indicibili complectebatur amore, eo quod Dominum maiestatis fratrem nobis effecerit et per eam simus misericordiam consecuti. In ipsa post Christum praecipue fidens, eam sui ac suorum advocatam constituit et ad honorem ipsius a festo Apostolorum Petri et Pauli usque ad festum Assumptionis devotissime ieiunabat.—Angelicis spiritibus ardentibus igne mirifice ad excedendum in Deum et electorum animas inflammandas inseparabilis erat amoris vinculo copulatus et ob devotionem ipsorum ab Assumptione Virginis gloriosae quadraginta diebus ieiunans orationi iugiter insistebat. Beato autem Michaeli archangelo, eo quod animarum repraesentandarum haberet officium, speciali erat amore devotior propter fervidum quem habebat zelum ad salutem omnium salvandorum.—Ex recordatione sanctorum omnium tamquam lapidum ignitorum in deificum recalescebat incendium, Apostolos omnes, et praecipue Petrum et Paulum, propter fervidam caritatem, quem habuerunt ad Christum, summa devotione complexans; ob quorum reverentiam et amorem quadragesimae specialis ieiunium Domino dedicabat. Non habebat aliud Christi pauper nisi dua minuta, corpus scilicet et animam, quae posset liberali caritate largiri. Sed haec per amorem Christi sic offerebat continue, ut quasi omni tempore per rigorem ieiunii corpus et per ardorem desiderii spiritum immolaret, exterius in atrio sacrificans holocaustum et in templo interius concremans thymiama." —S. Bonaventura, *Legenda Maior S. Francisci Assisiensis* (editio minor, ad Claras Aquas, Florentiae: ex Typographia Collegii S. Bonaventurae, 1941), pp. 75–76; Bartholomaeus de Pisa, *De Conformitate Vitae Beati Francisci ad Vitam Domini Iesu* (*Analecta Franciscana,* V, ad Claras Aquas prope Florentiam, 1906), p. 110; *Monumenta ad Constitutiones Ordinis Fratrum Minorum Capuccinorum Pertinentia* (Romae, 1916), pp. 184–185.

render it insipid by mixing it with ashes or by diluting it with water. Although, in keeping with the words of the Gospel,[3] he partook of whatever food was set before him when traveling, while at home he almost never ate meat. "What can I say of wine," wrote Saint Bonaventure, "when he hardly took enough water to slake his burning thirst?" Day by day, he sought out new ways in which to mortify his body in the use of food and drink.[4]

When the *Fioretti* open by saying: "First let us consider how the life of the glorious Saint Francis was conformed in every act to that of our Blessed Lord," [5] they indicate the underlying reason why Francis subjected himself to such severe fasts:—his unquenchable desire to be perfectly conformed to Christ. Francis wanted to be like Christ in all things, and fasting was one of the principal means he used to reach his ideal. Francis fasted in order to drive from his members anything that could be an obstacle to his perfect conformity to Christ. Francis also fasted because Christ had given him the example by his own fast. Fasting made Francis like Christ.

Love was at the root of Saint Francis' intense desire to imitate Christ. Love is the key to the spirit of fasting in the Franciscan Order. A Franciscan's love for Christ should make his fasting a thing of joy. Love for Christ should urge Franciscans not merely to observe the obligatory fasts of the Church and of the Rule. It should move them to do something more, because true love knows no limits in its ways of expression. Love for Christ should impel Franciscans voluntarily to follow the example of their Seraphic Father in observing the "Lent of Benediction" and the other fasts which he was wont to keep.[6]

Christ influenced the early Christians to practice fasting, not so much by command as by example.[7] Francis wished to do the same

[3] Luke, 10:8.

[4] S. Bonaventura, *Legenda Maior,* pp. 38–39; Thomas de Celano, *Vita Prima S. Francisci Assisiensis* (ad Claras Aquas prope Florentiam, 1926), n. 51.

[5] *The Little Flowers of St. Francis of Assisi* (New York: Catholic Book Publishing Co., 1950), p. 9.

[6] *Constitutiones Fratrum Minorum Capuccinorum, 1925* (editio altera, Romae, Typis Polyglottis Vaticanis, 1931), n. 69.

[7] Herrera, *Legislación Eclesiástica sobre el Ayuno y la Abstinencia,* pp. 12–13.

for his followers. He wanted them to follow his example as he had followed the example furnished by Christ. He wanted them to fast, not so much from compulsion as from love, a love that would make them, like him, perfect imitators of Christ.

Article II. Early Franciscan Legislation on Fast and Abstinence

Extant sources of information concerning the earliest Franciscan discipline on fast and abstinence are very few. The text of the primitive Rule, which was approved by Pope Innocent III on April 16, 1209, has disappeared.[8] Similarly, the enactments of the General Chapters that were held during the first years of the Order have been lost.[9] The oldest available primary sources are the so-called *Regula Prima,* which Saint Francis wrote in 1221, and the *Regula Secunda,* which is also called the *Regula Bullata.* Although the *Regula Prima* never received papal approval,[10] it is valuable in that it conveys an insight into the Saint's mind on fasting at the time when it was written. The *Regula Bullata,* which received the approbation of Pope Honorius III on the twenty-ninth of November in 1223,[11] remains to our own day as the fundamental law of the Franciscan Order.

There exist, nevertheless, in other ancient works scattered references to legislation in the Order on fast and abstinence prior to the composition of the *Regula Prima* in 1221. The *Chronicle of Brother Jordan,*[12] for example, tells us that, in the year 1219,[13]

---

[8] Quaglia, *L'Originalità della Regola Francescana* (Sassoferrato: Scuola Tipografica Francescana, 1942), pp. 1–13; Robinson, "Quo Anno Ordo Fratrum Minorum Inceperit," *Archivum Franciscanum Historicum,* II (1909), 181–196; Holzapfel, *Manuale Historiae Ordinis Fratrum Minorum* (Latine redditum a Haselbeck, Friburgi Brisgoviae, 1909), p. 16; Cuthbert, *Life of St. Francis of Assisi* (New York, 1921), p. 465.

[9] Quaglia, *L' Originalità della Regola Francescana,* pp. 13–15.

[10] Holzapfel, *Manuale Historiae Ordinis Fratrum Minorum,* p. 18.

[11] *Seraphicae Legislationis Textus Originales* (ad Claras Aquas prope Florentiam, 1897), p. 47.

[12] "Beatus autem Franciscus cum beato Petro Cathanie, iuris perito et domino legum, mare transiens reliquit duos vicarios, fratrem Matheum de Narnio et fratrem Gregorium de Neapoli, Matheum vero instituit ad sanctam Mariam de Porciuncula, ut ibi manens recipiendos ad ordinem reciperet, Gregorium autem, ut circuiendo Ytaliam fratres consolaretur. Et quia

the legislation [14] of the Order: 1) prescribed fasting on Wednesdays and Fridays; 2) with the permission of Saint Francis, allowed the Friars to fast on Mondays and Saturdays; and 3) granted the liberty of eating meat on all days that were not days of abstinence. Since it was the general practice of the time, there can be no doubt that the Friars added to the foregoing the observance also of the "Lents" before Christmas and Easter.[15]

The *Regula Prima* of 1221 greatly simplified and mitigated the earlier legislation in the Order by ordaining that the Friars should fast: 1) from the Feast of All Saints until Christmas; 2) from the Feast of the Epiphany until Easter; and 3) on all Fridays of the year.[16]

The *Regula Bullata* of 1223 tempered even further the Franciscan legislation on fasting. It repeated the ordinances of the

---

secundum primam regulam fratres feria quarta et VI et per licentiam beati Francisci feria secunda et sabato ieiunabant et omni carnali feria carnes comedebant, isti vicarii cum quibusdam fratribus senioribus Ytaliae unum capitulum celebrarunt, in quo statuerunt, ut fratres diebus carnalibus carnibus procuratis non uterentur, sed tantum sponte a fidelibus oblatas manducarent. Et insuper statuerunt, ut feriam secundam ieiunarent cum aliis duobus diebus, et ut feria secunda et sabato sibi lacticinia non procurarent, sed ab eis abstinerent, nisi forte a devotis fidelibus offerrentur."—*Chronica Fratris Jordani* (ed. H. Boehmer, Parisiis, 1908), n. 11.

[13] Angelus of Clareno placed the journey spoken of by Brother Jordan in the thirteenth year of the conversion of Saint Francis, or the year 1219—Angelus Clarenus, *Expositio Regulae Fratrum Minorum* (ed. L. Oliger, ad Claras Aquas, 1912), p. 7.

[14] For the nature of this legislation, see: Nicholas of Cork, *Fast and Abstinence in Franciscan Legislation* (Rome: Pontificia Universitas Gregoriana, 1943), pp. 13–15; Huber, *A Documented History of the Franciscan Order* (Milwaukee: Nowiny, 1944), p. 12; Fidel de Pamplona, "Ayunos y Abstinencias en la Regla Franciscana," *Ius Seraphicum,* I (1955), p. 274.

[15] Herrera, *Legislación Eclesiástica sobre el Ayuno y la Abstinencia,* pp. 43–44; p. 61.

[16] "Et similiter omnes fratres ieiunent a festo omnium sanctorum usque ad Natale Domini et ab Epiphania, quando Dominus noster Iesus Christus incepit ieiunare, usque ad Pascha; alias autem temporibus non teneantur secundum hanc vitam nisi sexta feria ieiunare. Et liceat eis manducare de omnibus cibis, qui apponuntur eis, secundum Evangelium."—*Opuscula Sancti Patris Francisci* (ad Claras Aquas prope Florentiam; ex Typographia Collegii S. Bonaventurae, 1949), p. 29.

Regula Prima that the Friars must fast: 1) from the Feast of All Saints until Christmas; and 2) on all Fridays of the year. But it revoked the ordinance which imposed a fast from the Epiphany until Easter. In its place: 1) it instituted the so-called "Lent of Benediction," a fast of forty days following the Feast of the Epiphany, whose observance was left to the voluntary choice of the Friars; and 2) it repeated the precept, already binding from the general law, that the Friars must fast during the Lent before Easter.[17]

The gradual relaxation of the primitive rigor of the legislation on fast and abstinence in the Order within the very lifetime of Saint Francis is striking. It emphasizes the definite break which the Saint made with traditional monasticism.[18] It also betrays the influence of his personal spiritual progress on the development of the legislation of the Order. As he advanced in holiness, he more and more made love for Christ the sole motive for all his actions. In mitigating the prescriptions of the Rule on fast and abstinence, he showed that he wanted his Friars to be like himself. He wanted love for Christ and not legal enactments to be the motive for their works of penance. He did not lessen the demands of the Rule because he expected the Friars to fast less often. He did so because he expected them to fast voluntarily from a motive of pure love for Christ.

In comparison with other religious Orders of his time, Francis demanded very little of his followers. The Benedictines, the Premonstratensians, the Carthusians, the Carmelites, and the Dominicans, for example, were all obliged to fast from the Feast of the Exaltation of the Holy Cross on September 14 until Easter. The Dominicans and Carmelites were further obliged to fast on all

[17] "Et ieiunent a festo omnium sanctorum usque ad Nativitatem Domini. Sanctam vero quadragesimam, quae incipit ab Epiphania usque ad continuos quadraginta dies, quam Dominus suo sancto ieiunio consecravit, qui voluntarie eam ieiunant, benedicti sint a Domino, et qui nolunt, non sint adstricti. Sed aliam usque ad Resurrectionem Domini ieiunent. Aliis autem temporibus non teneantur, nisi sexta feria, ieiunare. Tempore vero manifestae necessitatis non teneantur fratres ieiunio corporali."—*Opuscula Sancti Patris Francisci*, p. 66.

[18] Felder, *The Ideals of St. Francis of Assisi*, tr. Berchmans Bittle (New York, 1925), p. 225; Nicholas of Cork, *Fast and Abstinence in Franciscan Legislation*, p. 13.

Fridays of the year. The Carthusians were bound to fast on Mondays and Fridays.[19] Saint Bonaventure (1221–1274) offered a reason for the comparative leniency of Franciscan legislation on fasting. It was simply that Saint Francis found very little in the Gospels on fasting.[20] The ideals of the Order lay not in human traditions, but in Christ.

Francis' ideal of conformity to Christ made him not only very mild in his legislation on fast and abstinence, it made him also very brief. As he reasoned, the Friars' fervent zeal to conform their lives perfectly to Christ's would render detailed instructions and regulations unnecessary and superfluous. Their love for Christ and their ideal would supply for any deficiency of detail in the Rule.

History does not completely bear out the Saint's hopes. Few of those who came to the Order lived with the same singleness of purpose as Francis. Even if some did, in a given circumstance each might have his own idea of what conformity to Christ implied. This could be disastrous for the common life. Sincere and saintly men who strove to live in strict accordance with the Franciscan Rule as the surest means of reaching Christian perfection found great difficulty in relating the general character of its legislation to the specific contingencies of daily life.

When Francis went overseas in the year 1219 and appointed Matthew of Narni and Gregory of Naples to be his vicars, it might very well have been this difficult situation that prompted them to enact further legislation dealing with fast and abstinence. But Francis would have none of it. As soon as he heard of it, he repudiated it. His Friars were to live the Gospel. To do so, they had to be free in the service and in the love of God. They could not be fettered by an abundance of minute and hampering regulations.[21]

---

[19] Fidel de Pamplona, "Ayunos y Abstinencias en la Regla Franciscana," *IS*, I (1955), 270–271.

[20] "Quodsi quaeras, quare tam parum ieiunii imposuit Fratribus observandum? respondeo, quod . . . de ieiunio disciplinae parum reperit sanctus Franciscus in Evangelio expressum. . . ."—S. Bonaventura, "Expositio super Regulam Fratrum Minorum," *Opera Omnia* (ad Claras Aquas prope Florentiam, 1898), VIII, 410.

[21] "Super quibus constitucionibus, eo quod presumpserant aliquid addere

Nevertheless, soon after the death of Saint Francis it became clear that, if the Order was to survive, supplementary legislation would have to be enacted to serve as an adaptation of both the spirit and the letter of the Rule to constantly changing circumstances. It was for this reason that, by the authority of the Holy See, Constitutions came to be introduced into the Order.[22]

Originally the entirety of Franciscan discipline on fast and abstinence was embodied in the Rule. But in consequence of the long process of growth and development that it underwent, it later came to be scattered. New and important dispositions came into force from various sources. Many of these dispositions found their way into the Constitutions, with the result that today the greater part of the Order's law on fast and abstinence is contained either in the Rule or in the Constitutions. Others, however, have not been incorporated into the Constitutions. They still oblige as they were first issued. They are to be found in the various acts of the Holy See which touch on the Order, and in a number of decisions and instructions of authorities within the Order.

Article III. Prescribed Times of Fast

The Franciscan Rule ordains that the Friars shall fast: 1) from the Feast of All Saints until Christmas; 2) during the Lent that

regule sancti patris, quidam frater laycus indignatus assumptis secum illis constitucionibus sine licentia vicariorum transfretavit. Et ad beatum Franciscum veniens in primis culpam suam coram ipso dixit veniam petens super eo, quod ad ipsum sine licentia accessisset hac necessitate inductus, quod vicarii, quos reliquerat, super suam regulam novas leges adicere presumpsissent, insuper adiciens, quod ordo per totam Ytaliam turbaretur tam per vicarios quam per alios fratres nova presumentes. Constitucionibus perlectis cum beatus Franciscus esset in mensa et carnes appositas ad manducandum coram se haberet, dixit fratri Petro: 'Domine Petre, quid faciemus?' Et ille respondit: 'Ha, domine Francisce, quod vobis placet, quia potestatem habetis vos.' Et quia frater Petrus vir litteratus erat et nobilis, beatus Franciscus propter suam urbanitatem ipsum honorando dominum appellavit . . . Et hec mutua reverencia fuit inter ipsos tam ultra mare quam in Ytalia. Et sic tandem beatus Franciscus intulit: 'Comedamus ergo secundum ewangelium que nobis apponuntur.' "—*Chronica Fratris Jordani*, n. 12.

[22] Bernardino da Siena, *Esposizione della Regola Francescana* (Firenze: Curia Provincializia dei Frati Minori Cappuccini, 1950), n. 1; n. 27; Albertus a Bulsano, *Expositio Regulae FF. Minorum* (Rome: 1932), n. 1.

precedes our Lord's Resurrection; 3) on all Fridays. Besides these positive prescriptions, the Rule concedes the following liberties: 1) that those who wish may keep the "Lent of Benediction;" and 2) that the Friars are not obliged to fast in cases of manifest necessity. Finally, the Rule states that at other times the Friars shall not be obliged to fast.[23] In the pages which follow, each of the foregoing prescriptions will in turn be discussed and explained.

Article IV. The "Lent" That Precedes Christmas

During the early centuries of Christianity, the practice was widespread among the faithful of sanctifying the period before Christmas by a solemn fast.[24] By the twelfth century, however, the practice had fallen into desuetude in many places.[25] But Saint Francis was unwilling to see it disappear among his Friars. His intense devotion to the Christchild moved him to renew and to confirm this ancient observance in the Order with a special precept of the Rule. In the third chapter, he writes: "And the Friars shall fast from the Feast of All Saints until Christmas."[26] Pope Clement V (1305–1314) in the decretal *Exivi* listed this command of Saint Francis as one of the equivalent precepts of the Rule.[27]

Although the wording of the Rule might possibly be interpreted in such a manner as to include the two feast days, All Saints and Christmas, within the "Lent," the expositors of the Franciscan

[23] "Et ieiunent a festo omnium sanctorum usque ad Nativitatem Domini. Sanctam vero quadragesimam, quae incipit ab Epiphania usque ad continuos quadraginta dies, quam Dominus suo sancto ieiunio consecravit, qui voluntarie eam ieiunant, benedicti sint a Domino, et qui nolunt, non sint adstricti. Sed aliam usque ad Resurrectionem Domini ieiunent. Aliis autem temporibus non teneantur, nisi sexta feria, ieiunare. Tempore vero manifestae necessitatis non teneantur fratres ieiunio corporali."—*Opuscula Sancti Patris Francisci,* p. 66.

[24] Wernz-Vidal, *Ius Canonicum* (7 vols., Vol. IV, Romae: Apud Aedes Universitatis Gregorianae, 1934–1935), n. 524; Herrera, *Legislación Eclesiástica sobre el Ayuno y la Abstinencia,* pp. 59–62.

[25] Herrera, *Legislación Eclesiástica sobre el Ayuno y la Abstinencia,* p. 61.

[26] "Et ieiunent a festo omnium sanctorum usque ad Nativitatem Domini." —*Opuscula Sancti Patris Francisci,* p. 66.

[27] *Seraphicae Legislationis Textus Originales,* p. 237.

Rule are unanimously agreed in teaching that the fast begins only on November 2 and ends on the vigil of Christmas.[28]

Article V. The Lent that Precedes Our Lord's Resurrection

The Franciscan Rule states of the Lent preceding our Lord's Resurrection: "Sed aliam (quadragesimam) usque ad Resurrectionem Domini ieiunent." [29] The Rule's use of the subjunctive mode of the verb *ieiunent* indicates an obligation. There is no doubt that the Friars are bound to observe the Lent spoken of. But the Rule does not clearly determine the source of the obligation. Hence the question arises:—Does the Rule merely call the attention of the Friars to the previously existing obligation incumbent upon them from Church law to keep that fast; or does it impose a new and distinct obligation?

The answer to this question will be found from a close study of: 1) the Rule itself; 2) the papal decretal *Exivi;* 3) the intention of Saint Francis; 4) the Constitutions of the Order; and 5) the writings of the expositors of the Franciscan Rule.

Section 1. The Rule Itself

In order to ascertain what the Rule teaches about the source of the obligation for the Lent before Easter, one must take two points into careful consideration. The first is the meaning of a word. The second is the omission of a phrase. The word is *ieiunent,* which is used in the Rule. The phrase is *secundum hanc vitam,* which is omitted from the Rule.

IEIUNENT

When it speaks of the obligation of the fast before Christmas, and again when it speaks of the obligation of the fast before Easter, the Franciscan Rule uses exactly the same word:—*ieiunent.* In the one case the Rule states: "Et *ieiunent* a festo

---

[28] Albertus a Bulsano, *Expositio Regulae FF. Minorum,* n. 165.

[29] *Opuscula Sancti Patris Francisci,* p. 66: "But they shall fast during the other Lent which lasts until our Lord's Resurrection."

omnium sanctorum usque ad Nativitatem Domini." [30] In the other case the Rule states: "Sed aliam (quadragesimam) usque ad Resurrectionem Domini *ieiunent.*" [31]

The expressions used in reference to the two obligations are strikingly parallel. But grammatical parallelism of expression alone does not necessarily imply a parallelism of meaning and of obligation. The context must also be considered. In the matter under consideration, the context shows the distinct and equal possibility of an explanation at variance with that indicated by the grammatical parallelism, an explanation that denies the presence of any parallelism of meaning or of obligation.

When the word *ieiunent* is used with reference to the fast before Christmas, it can have only one possible meaning. The subjunctive mode of the verb indicates an obligation. That obligation surely does not arise from the general law of the Church, because the general law does not prescribe fast during that season. It can only indicate the direct imposition of an obligation by the Rule.

When the word *ieiunent* is used with reference to the fast before Easter, the situation is quite different. The Lent before Easter is of obligation for all Christians from general Church law. In this situation the obligation indicated by the subjunctive mode of the verb can be verified in either of two ways. It can indicate the imposition of a new and special precept of the Rule, in parallel with the precept to fast before Christmas; or it can simply indicate to the Friars that they are bound by the law of the Church to observe this Lent, without imposing a special obligation. Either explanation is possible from a consideration of the mere wording of the Rule. The solution to the difficulty must be sought elsewhere.

It is a rule of law that favorable laws are to be interpreted broadly and burdensome laws strictly.[32] Applied to the case at hand, this rule demands that the meaning of *ieiunent* be interpreted strictly. It demands that it be taken to mean that the Franciscan

---

[30] *Opuscula Sancti Patris Francisci,* p. 66: "And the Friars shall fast from the Feast of All Saints until Christmas."

[31] *Opuscula Sancti Patris Francisci,* p. 66: "But they shall fast during the other Lent which lasts until our Lord's Resurrection."

[32] "Odia restringi et favores convenit ampliari."—Reg. 15, R. J., in VI°.

Rule merely recalls the obligation of the common law to fast before Easter without imposing a new obligation of its own.

SECUNDUM HANC VITAM

The significance of the phrase *secundum hanc vitam* [33] is found in its omission from the *Regula Bullata* after Saint Francis had earlier used it in the *Regula Prima.* The corresponding passages from the two redactions of the Rule are identical, except for the presence of the phrase in the earlier redaction and its absence in the later. The pertinent passage in the *Regula Prima* reads: "Aliis autem temporibus non teneantur *secundum hanc vitam* nisi sexta feria ieiunare." [34] That same passage in the *Regula Bullata* reads: "Aliis autem temporibus non teneantur, nisi sexta feria, ieiunare." [35]

The reason for the omission of the phrase in the *Regula Bullata* can be gathered from a study of the third chapters of both redactions of the Rule. When the Rule states that at other times the Friars shall not be bound to fast, the question that naturally comes to mind is:—other than what? The Rule itself supplies the answer. In a general way it is this:—at times other than those stated in the Rule. But different times are stated in the two redactions of the Rule. Therefore each redaction will have its own specific answer. And these answers, in turn, will supply the reason for the omission of the *secundum hanc vitam* in the *Regula Bullata.*

The *Regula Prima* declares that the Friars are bound to fast: 1) from the Feast of All Saints until Christmas; and 2) from the Feast of the Epiphany until Easter. Neither of these fasts is prescribed by general Church law. Both are of obligation solely from the Franciscan Rule. Inasmuch as they oblige solely from the Rule, or according to the Franciscan way of life, the *Regula Prima,* when referring to them, accurately states that at other times the Friars shall not be bound to fast *secundum hanc vitam.*

---

[33] "According to this life."

[34] *Opuscula Sancti Patris Francisci,* p. 29: "At other times they shall not be bound to fast according to this life except on Fridays."

[35] *Opuscula Sancti Patris Francisci,* p. 66: "At other times they shall not be bound to fast except on Fridays."

The *Regula Bullata,* however, declares that the Friars are bound to fast: 1) from the Feast of All Saints until Christmas; and 2) during the Lent which precedes Easter. Unlike the fasts imposed by the *Regula Prima,* both of which are of obligation only from the Rule, one of these fasts obliges from the common law. The *Regula Bullata* could have reimposed this fast by way of a special precept, or it could have been content with simply recalling it as already binding from the common law. The omission of the phrase *secundum hanc vitam* indicates that it chose the latter alternative. The presence of the phrase in the *Regula Bullata* would have indicated that both fasts were imposed according to the Franciscan way of life, or by way of a special precept of the Rule. Its omission can mean only one thing, namely, the Lent preceding Easter is not imposed *secundum hanc vitam.* It obliges only in virtue of the general law.[36]

Section 2. The Decretal EXIVI

The Franciscan Rule, in common with the Rules of other religious Orders, has received the highest possible papal approbation. Theologians teach that the Church acts infallibly when it solemnly approves the Rule of a religious Order.[37] Canonists would say that the approbation was granted *in forma specifica.* In a juridic sense, therefore, in so far as the Rule is law, its author is the Holy See;[38] and, consequently, only the Holy See can interpret it in an authentic manner.[39]

One of the most important authentic interpretations of the Rule

---

[36] Cf. Nicholas of Cork, *Fast and Abstinence in Franciscan Legislation,* pp. 19–21.

[37] Hervé, *Manuale Theologiae Dogmaticae* (4 vols., Vol. I, Parisiis: apud Berche et Pagis, Editores, 1949), nn. 520, 521.

[38] Goyeneche, *Quaestiones Canonicae de Iure Religiosorum* (2 vols., Neapoli: M. d'Auria, Pontificius Editor, 1954–1955), I, p. 89; Matthaeus Conte a Coronata, *Institutiones Iuris Canonici* (5 vols., Vol. I, 4 ed., Romae, Taurini: Marietti, 1950), n. 507 (hereafter cited *Institutiones*).

[39] *Constitutiones Generales Ordinis Fratrum Minorum, 1953* (Romae: Curia Generalis Ordinis, 1953), art. 1; *Constitutiones Ordinis Fratrum Minorum Sancti Patris Francisci Conventualium, 1932* (Romae: ad SS. XII Apostolos, 1932), n. 10; *Constitutiones Fratrum Minorum Capuccinorum, 1925,* n. 3.

that the Order has ever received is the decretal *Exivi*, which the Holy See, in the person of Pope Clement V, issued at the third and final session of the Council of Vienne on May 6, 1312.[40] Parts of the decretal directly concern the Rule's legislation on fasting.

The purpose of the *Exivi* was to ease the consciences of the Friars by clarifying some of the obscurity in the wording of the Rule.[41] Some years before, on August 14, 1279, Pope Nicholas III had issued his famous bull *Exiit*, in which he had declared that the Friars were bound to the observance of those evangelical counsels which were expressed by the Rule: 1) as formal precepts; 2) as formal inhibitions; or 3) in words equivalent to precepts.[42]

Unfortunately, the practical application of these norms was not so clear as their theoretical divisions might indicate. Pope Clement V even said of the bull of his predecessor that it increased rather than lessened difficulties.[43] The precise difficulties that the Friars

[40] Holzapfel, *Manuale Historiae Ordinis Fratrum Minorum*, p. 52. For the complete text, see: *Seraphicae Legislationis Textus Originales*, pp. 229–260.

[41] "Quia vero dictae sanctae Regulae professores ac aemulatores devoti, ut alumni et veri filii tanti patris, affectabant sicut et ferventer affectant ad purum et plenum promissam Regulam firmiter observare; attendentes quaedam, quae dubium poterant afferre sensum, in ipsius Regulae serie contineri, pro ipsorum declaratione habenda recurrerunt prudenter olim ad apicem Apostolicae dignitatis, ut certificati per ipsam, *cuius pedibus etiam per ipsam Regulam sunt subjecti*, possent Domino, pulsis cunctis dubiis, cum plena claritate conscientiae deservire."—*Seraphicae Legislationis Textus Originales*, pp. 230–231.

[42] ". . . non fuit loquentis (Sancti Francisci) intentio quod Fratres ex professione hujus Regulae ad omnia consilia sicut ad praecepta Evangelica tenerentur, sed solum ad illa consilia quae in eadem Regula praeceptorie vel inhibitorie seu sub verbis aequipollentibus sunt expressa."—*Seraphicae Legislationis Textus Originales*, p. 189.

[43] "Et quia, ut intelleximus, non minuitur nunc hoc dubium, sed augetur ex eo quod felicis recordationis Nicolaus Papa tertius praedecessor Noster noscitur declarasse quod Fratres ipsi ex professione suae Regulae sunt adstricti ad ea consilia evangelica quae in ipsa Regula praeceptorie vel inhibitorie, seu sub verbis aequipollentibus exprimuntur, et nihilominus ad eorum omnium observantiam quae ipsis in eadem Regula sub verbis obligatoriis indicuntur: supplicaverunt praedicti Fratres, ut ad ipsorum conscientias serenandas declarare quae eorum censeri debeant praeceptis aequipollentia ac obligatoria dignaremur."—*Seraphicae Legislationis Textus Originales*, p. 236.

encountered were concerned with the so-called equivalent precepts of the Rule. These were precepts which the Rule proposed, not in a formal way, but by using words that were equivalently preceptive. The Friars quite readily understood the Rule's meaning when it was formally preceptive or formally inhibitory; but they did not quite so readily grasp its meaning when it was equivalently preceptive. Many of the difficulties concerned matters that were of the greatest consequence for the regular observance. Unless they were settled, the pure and conscientious observance of the Rule would be impossible. Pope Clement was determined to give a solution to the unfortunate situation and to clear up the doubts which were troubling the consciences of the Friars.

His purpose dictated his method, because his solution was essentially casuistic. Although he spoke of certain fundamental principles which might serve as a guide in determining just when the wording of the Rule determined the force of a precept,[44] he treated these principles in so general and disconnected a way that, as they stand in the *Exivi,* they could never serve as a practical norm of conduct. Nor did he intend them as such. He used them rather by way of explanation than by way of command.

The Pope's real answer to the difficulty followed his discussion of the principles. Here he no longer simply explained. He descended to specific cases. He furnished a clear and definite enumeration of the equivalent precepts to which the Friars were bound if they wanted to observe the Rule in all its purity and rigor.[45]

---

[44] ". . . dicimus quod licet Fratres non ad omnium quae sub verbis imperativi modi ponuntur in Regula, sicut ad praeceptorum seu praeceptis aequipollentium observantiam teneantur, expedit tamen ipsis Fratribus, ad observandam puritatem Regulae et rigorem, quod ad ea sicut ad aequipollentia praeceptis se noverint obligatos, quae hic inferius annotantur."—*Seraphicae Legislationis Textus Originales,* pp. 236–237.

[45] "Ut autem haec, quae videri possunt aequipollentia praeceptis ex vi verbi, vel saltem ratione materiae de qua agitur, seu ex utroque, sub compendio habeantur, declaramus quod illud quod ponitur in Regula:

De non habendo plures tunicas quam unam cum capucio, et aliam sine capucio;

item, *de non portandis calceamentis, et de non equitando extra casum necessitatis;*

The Pope's purpose was clearly to dispel the Friars' doubts of conscience. He wished them no longer to be troubled with the uncertainties that come from vague and indefinite principles. In the *Exivi* he gave them a complete and orderly list of the equivalent precepts which they were bound to observe.

When speaking of fasting, the *Exivi* states that the Rule proposes the following as an equivalent precept: "that they (the Friars) are bound to fast from the Feast of All Saints until the Nativity of the Lord, and on Fridays." [46] The decretal states nothing about the Lent before Easter. In view of the express purpose of the *Exivi,* it is inconceivable that the Pope could have overlooked it. In view of that same purpose, it is equally inconceivable to imagine that he mentioned it in some vague implicit way. His purpose was to settle doubts, not to create them. The

---

item, quod *Fratres vilibus induantur;*

item, quod *jejunare a festo omnium Sanctorum usque ad Natale Domini et in sextis feriis teneantur;*

item, quod *Clerici faciant divinum Officium secundum ordinem sanctae Romanae Ecclesiae;*

item, quod *Ministri et Custodes pro necessitatibus infirmorum et Fratribus induendis solicite curam gerant;*

item, quod *si quis Fratrum in infirmitatem ceciderit, alii Fratres debent ei servire;*

item, quod *Fratres non praedicent in episcopatu alicujus Episcopi, cum ab eo illis fuerit contradictum;*

item, quod *nullus audeat penitus populo praedicare, nisi a generali Ministro,* vel aliis quibus secundum declarationem praedictam id competit, *fuerit examinatus, approbatus, et ad hoc institutus;*

item, quod *Fratres qui cognoscerent se non posse Regulam spiritualiter observare, debeant et possint ad suos Ministros recurrere;*

item, omnia quae ponuntur in Regula, ad formam habitus tam novitiorum quam etiam professorum, nec non et ad modum receptionis, ad professionem spectantia, nisi recipientibus quoad habitum novitiorum, sicut dicit Regula, secundum Deum aliter videatur: haec, inquam, omnia sunt a Fratribus tanquam obligatoria observanda;

item, Ordo communiter sensit, tenet et tenuit ab antiquo quod ubicumque ponitur in Regula hoc vocabulum *teneantur,* obtinet vim praecepti, et servari debet a Fratribus sicut tale."—*Seraphicae Legislationis Textus Originales,* pp. 237-238.

[46] ". . . quod ieiunare a festo omnium Sanctorum usque ad Natale Domini et in sextis feriis teneantur."—*Seraphicae Legislationis Textus Originales,* p. 237.

only reasonable explanation for its omission is that there is no special precept of the Rule to fast before Easter.

Pope Clement made one other reference to fasting in the decretal when he declared: "Besides the two times mentioned in the Rule during which they are bound to fast, namely, from the Feast of all Saints until the Nativity of our Lord and the great Lent, it is further stated in the same Rule: At other times they shall not be bound to fast except on Fridays." [47] In this passage the Pope was directly concerned with the obligation of the Friars to fast at other times of the year. By way of developing his explanation he made reference to the fast before Christmas and that before Easter. Since he had already furnished a lengthy and precise solution for the problems concerned with the equivalent precepts of the Rule earlier in the decretal, he was careful to avoid the use of any expressions that might tend to obscure that solution. When speaking of the two fasts referred to by the Rule, he spoke of them as *annotatis in Regula,* as mentioned in the Rule, not as prescribed by the Rule. Thus he preserved the clarity of his earlier explanation that only the fast before Christmas is binding from a special precept of the Rule, while the Lent before Easter is of obligation solely from Church law.

Pope Clement V concluded his enumeration of the equivalent precepts of the Rule by declaring that "wherever the word '*teneantur*' is used in the Rule, it obtains the force of a precept." [48] Some expositors of the Rule [49] see in this an argument that the Lent before Easter binds in virtue of the Rule, for the Rule

---

[47] ". . . cum duobus temporibus annotatis in Regula, scilicet a festo omnium Sanctorum usque ad Nativitatem Domini, et maximae Quadragesimae, in quibus ieiunare tenentur, inseratur in eadem Regula: Aliis autem temporibus non teneantur nisi sexta feria ieiunare."—*Seraphicae Legislationis Textus Originales,* p. 242.

[48] ". . . ubicumque ponitur in Regula hoc vocabulum 'teneantur,' obtinet vim praecepti."—*Seraphicae Legislationis Textus Originales,* p. 238.

[49] Antonius M. de Corduba, *Expositio Evangelicae Regulae Seraphici Patris Sancti Francisci* (Venetiis, 1610), p. 152; Hieronymus a Politio, *Expositio cum Dubiis Excussis in Regulam Seraphici Patriarchae S. Francisci* (Neapoli, 1606), p. 291, (hereafter cited *Expositio*); Santi Thesauro Romano, *Espositione sopra la Regola del Seráfico Padre S. Francesco* (Roma, 1614), p. 161.

states: "At other times they shall not be bound to fast except on Fridays," [50] using the Latin verb form *non teneantur.*

This passage from the Rule has some reference to the fasts which were mentioned previously. It refers to them in this wise: that the Friars shall not be bound to fast at times other than those mentioned in the Rule. The *Exivi* declared that, when the word *teneantur* is used in the Rule, it obtains the force of a precept. In this case it is the phrase *non teneantur* which is used. The Rule is not imposing an obligation here. On the contrary, it is freeing the Friars from the obligation to fast at other times. Furthermore, when the Rule is actually stating the obligation of the Friars to keep the two fasts which it mentions, it uses the word *ieiunent* in both cases, and not the word *teneantur.*

Some authors try to find an indication that the Rule proposes a special precept to observe the Lent before Easter in Pope Clement's failure to include among the equivalent precepts the obligation incumbent upon Franciscan lay brothers to recite seventy-six Our Fathers as their daily Divine Office.[51] If this omission on the Pope's part proves anything, it is this: that, unless there is some other way of establishing the obligation, Franciscan lay brothers are not bound to say their particular Office by a special precept of the Rule.[52]

Section 3. The Intention of Saint Francis

If Saint Francis wished to oblige his Friars by a special precept of the Rule to observe the Lent before Easter, it must be presumed that he had a motive for doing so. It cannot be presumed that he acted with complete arbitrariness. He need not have expressly stated that motive; but it had to exist. And if it did exist, it must be somehow discernible.

---

[50] "Aliis autem temporibus non teneantur nisi sexta feria ieiunare."—*Opuscula Sancti Patris Francisci,* p. 66.

[51] Nicholas of Cork, *Fast and Abstinence in Franciscan Legislation,* p. 22.

[52] Confer regarding this obligation: Kazenberger-Iglesias, *Liber Vitae* (Romae: Pontificium Athenaeum Antonianum, 1954), pp. 96–99; Albertus a Bulsano, *Expositio Regulae FF. Minorum,* n. 161; Bernardino da Siena, *Esposizione della Regola Francescana,* n. 349; Gabriel-Angelo da Vicenza-Cosmas Sartori, *La Regola dei Frati Minori* (Vincenza: Commisariato Terz'Ordine Francescano, 1937), pp. 102–105.

According to the teaching of the commentators on the Rule, only two practical consequences could have resulted from Saint Francis' proposing a special precept to keep the Lent before Easter: 1) the Friars younger than twenty-one and older than fifty-eight would be bound to observe that Lent; and 2) the Friars could not make use of dispensations from the Church fast granted by the Holy See or by local ordinaries. The Saint's motive, therefore, if he had one, would have had to be directed to one or both of these consequences. But nowhere did Saint Francis give the slightest indication that he gave thought to either of them. One searches in vain for any motive that could have moved him to impose this Lent by a special precept of the Rule. In the absence of such a motive, one cannot reasonably hold to the existence of a special precept. The only reasonable conclusion is that the Friars are obliged to observe the lent before Easter, not by the Rule, but purely in virtue of the common law.

Section 4. The Constitutions of the Order

Most of the Constitutions of the Order do not expressly enter into the question of the source of the obligation for the Lent before Easter. Some few, nevertheless, treat the subject with sufficient clarity to be of considerable help towards indicating a solution to the question.

The *Constitutiones Narbonenses* prefix their discussion of fasting with the words: "Since, according to the Rule, we are bound to observe two Lents . . ."[53] This same phrase is found repeated again and again in various of the Constitutions of the Order even as late as the seventeenth century.[54] Some authors hold that the words show that the obligation of the Lent preceding

---

[53] "Cum secundum Regulam teneamur duas quadragesimas ieiunare . . ." —*AFH*, XXXIV (1941), 55–56.

[54] "Constitutiones Assisienses, 1279," *AFH*, XXXIV (1941), 59; "Constitutiones Parisienses, 1292," *AFH*, XXXIV (1941), 59; "Constitutiones Assisienses, 1316," *AFH*, IV (1911), 282; "Statuta Caturcensia, 1337," *AFH*, XXX, (1937), 132; "Constitutiones Assisienses, 1340," *AFH*, VI, (1913), 259; "Statuta Lugdunensia, 1351," *AFH*, XXX, (1937), 163; "Constitutiones Farineriae, 1354," *AFH*, XXXV, (1942), 97; "Constitutiones Barcinonenses, 1451," *AFH*, XXXVIII (1945), 133; *Constitutiones Segovienses* (Segoviae, 1621), p. 641.

Easter arises from the Rule.[55] In point of fact, they really explain nothing. Whether the Easter Lent binds only from the common law or whether it binds also from the Rule, in either case the words of these Constitutions remain true, that "according to the Rule, we are bound to observe two Lents." The Constitutions simply make reference to the statement of the Rule, namely that the Friars are bound to keep the "Lents," without adding to it or explaining it. Like the Rule, the Constitutions make no direct reference to the source of the obligation.

The *Constitutiones Martinianae,* the twelfth general Constitutions of the Order, and published in 1430, are more specific.[56] Actually, they contain nothing completely new, but they are of great value in that they confirm the teaching of the *Exivi* on fasting exactly as it was originally promulgated. They incorporate the equivalent precepts of the Rule, word for word, as they stand in the *Exivi.* The *Constitutiones Martinianae* were published a century after the promulgation of the *Exivi.* Although they are a document of an essentially lower order than the papal decretal *Exivi,* and although their legislation could never, of itself, supplant the prescriptions of the *Exivi,* their authority is increased by the fact that they received papal approval. If any doubt had existed in the mind of Pope Martin V (1417–1431) concerning the obvious meaning of the precept on fasting in the *Exivi,*[57] or if that precept had been inaccurately worded, he surely would have remedied the situation on the occasion of his giving approval to the *Constitutiones Martinianae.* But he changed nothing. On the contrary, he ratified that precept just as it had first been written:—that the friars are bound to fast by an equivalent precept of the Rule during the "Lent" preceding Christmas and on Fridays. Like his predecessor, Pope Clement V, he makes no mention of an obligation from the Rule to fast during the Lent before Easter.

The *Constitutiones Alexandrinae,* drawn up by the General

---

[55] Nicholas of Cork, *Fast and Abstinence in Franciscan Legislation,* p. 21.

[56] Lucas Waddingus, *Annales Minorum* (27 vols., Vol. X, 3. ed., curavit Josephus Maria Fonseca, Ad Claras Aquas, 1932), p. 178.

[57] ". . . item, quod *ieiunare a festo omnium Sanctorum usque ad Natale Domini et in sextis feriis teneantur."—Seraphicae Legislationis Textus Originales,* p. 237.

Chapter of 1500, and published by apostolic authority in the following year, however, have caused trouble for certain authors.[58] These authors see in them an indication that there is a special precept of the Rule commanding fast during the Lent before Easter. The Constitutions read: "In the first place, it is ordained that the *precepts of the Rule* [59] concerning the two Lents are to be observed, one of which is common to all Christians, and the other peculiar to the Order of Friars Minor." [60] Viewed alone, and apart from the *Exivi,* the phrase *precepts of the Rule* in these Constitutions could seem to indicate that there exists a special precept concerning the Lent before Easter. But the *Constitutiones Alexandrinae* must be interpreted according to the *Exivi,* and not vice versa. Even though they received papal approval, they are substantially an act of the General Chapter of 1500. The *Exivi,* on the other hand, is an express authentic papal interpretation of the Franciscan Rule. When the *Exivi* speaks of the two "Lents," it speaks of them as *mentioned in the Rule.* Similarly here, when the *Constitutiones Alexandrinae* speak of the *precepts of the Rule,* they must be taken in this same sense. The expression *precepts of the Rule* must be understood to mean not *precepts imposed by the Rule,* but *precepts mentioned in the Rule.*

The *Constitutiones Generales Ordinis Fratrum Minorum* of 1953 have done much to clarify the situation. When they treat of fasting, they draw up a scheme of all the fasts to which the Friars are obliged, from whatever source. Under the heading *Ex iure communi,*[61] they list all the fasts to which the Friars are bound from the common law, including the Lent before Easter. Under the heading *Ex praecepto Regulae,*[62] they list all the fasts to which the Friars are bound by the Rule, without making mention

[58] Nicholas of Cork, *Fast and Abstinence in Franciscan Legislation,* p. 21; Piatus Montensis, *Praelectiones Juris Regularis* (3 vols., Vol. III, Parisiis: Casterman, 1900), p. 38.

[59] Italics are supplied by the writer.

[60] "Primo ordinatur, ut Regulae praecepta de duabus Quadragesimis observentur. Quarum una omnibus Christianis est communis, altera Fratribus Minoribus peculiaris."—De Gubernatis, *Orbis Seraphicus* (6 vols., Vols. I–V, Romae, 1682–1689; Vol. VI, ad Claras Aquas, 1886), III, 146.

[61] "From the common law."

[62] "From a precept of the Rule."

of the Lent before Easter as one of them. The conclusion which they force is indisputable: That Lent obliges only from the common law, and not also from the Rule.[63]

Section 5. The Teaching of the Expositors of the Rule

If the solution to the question concerning the existence of a special precept of the Rule to observe the Lent of the Church which precedes Easter were to be sought solely in the majority teaching of the expositors of the Rule, that solution would have to be in favor of the opinion which holds that the Rule imposes such a precept.

Among the early expositors of the Rule, Hugo a Digna (middle 13th century) is frequently cited as teaching the existence of this special precept, although his doctrine is not at all apparent from the text usually quoted.[64] Peter John Olivi (1248–1298),[65] Saint Bonaventure (1221–1274) [66] and the Minister General Gondisalvus a Vallebona (1304–1313),[67] however, were more explicit in their teaching, although none of them treated the problem as such.

[63] *Constitutiones Generales Ordinis Fratrum Minorum, 1953,* art. 181, § 1, n. 1; § 2.

[64] "Et ne putemus nos per hanc quadragesimam (i.e., Benedictionis) ab alia quam Ecclesia statuit eximi, subditur, 'Sed aliam usque ad resurrectionem Domini ieiunent.' "—"Expositio Fratris Hugonis super Regulam," Bonifatius a Ceva, *Speculum Minorum seu Firmamentum Trium Ordinum* (Venetiis, 1513), pars III, fol. 37.

[65] "Notate quod quadragesimam ab Ecclesia communiter iniunctam et celebratam hic nobis imponit. Tum ut per hoc doceret nos ieiunia et statuta Ecclesiae prae ceteris observare debere, tum quia non omnes sani communiter ad illam astringuntur, utpote secundum quosdam nonnisi post aetatis suae xxi annorum, et etiam quia posset in Ecclesia per diversas vias illud amoveri. Idcirco haec secunda voluit specialiter astringi."—"Declaratio Petri Ioannis super Regulam," Bonifatius a Ceva, *Speculum Minorum seu Firmamentum Trium Ordinum,* pars III, fol. 111.

[66] "Et (Sanctus Franciscus) loquitur de triplici quadragesima, duas praeceptorie imponens, tertium ad devotionis excitationem suadens."—"Expositio super Regulam Fratrum Minorum," *Opera Omnia,* VIII, 409.

[67] "Secundum est quod aliis temporibus praeterquam a festo omnium sanctorum usque ad nativitatem Domini et in quadragesima et sextis feriis non teneantur fratres ieiunare. Hoc est quod in supradictis teneantur, in aliis autem non si nolunt: et sic patet quod ieiunia Regulae aequipollent praecepto." —"Tractatus Fratris Gondisalvi de Praeceptis Regulae," Bonifatius a Ceva, *Speculum Minorum seu Firmamentum Trium Ordinum,* pars III, fol. 71.

From the sixteenth century onward, when the authors began to discuss the question professedly and at some length, the following expositors can be cited as teaching the existence of a special precept: Hieronymus a Politio,[68] Antonius de Corduba,[69] Emanuel Rodericus,[70] Santi Thesauro Romano,[71] Antonio da Patti,[72] Louis de Paris,[73] Petrus Marchant,[74] Giovanni Battista da Monza,[75] Bona-Gratia Habsensis,[76] Gaudentius Kerkhove,[77] Bernardinus von Gend,[78] Valerio do Sacramento,[79] Bernardo da Bologna,[80] Gabriel-Angelo da Vicenza,[81] Bonaventura Luchi,[82] Filippo di Castellucio,[83] Kilianus Kazenberger,[84] Gaudenzio da Brescia,[85]

---

68 *Expositio*, p. 289.

69 *Expositio Evangelicae Regulae Seraphici Patris Sancti Francisci*, p. 152.

70 *Quaestiones Regulares et Canonicae* (2 vols., Venetiis, 1611), II, 297–298.

71 *Espositione sopra la Regola del Seráfico Padre S. Francesco*, pp. 160–162.

72 *Considerationi et Espositioni sopra Tutti li Precetti della Regola de' Frati Minori* (Venetia, 1615), p. 242.

73 *Exposition Litterale de la Règle des FF. Mineurs* (Paris, 1623), pp. 194–195.

74 *Expositio Literalis in Regulam S. Francisci* (Antverpiae, 1631), p. 170; *Fundamenta Duodecim Ordinis Fratrum Minorum S. Francisci* (Bruxellis, 1657), p. 86.

75 *Espiacatione della Regola di San Francesco* (Napoli, 1647), pp. 226–227.

76 *Compendiosa Summula Selectarum Quaestionum Regularium* (Lugduni, 1671), n. 217.

77 *Commentarii in Generalia Statuta Ordinis S. Francisci Fratrum Minorum Provinciis Nationis Germano-Belgicae* (Coloniae Agrippinae, 1709), pp. 83–84.

78 *Ausslegung ueber die Regel der Minderbrueder* (Coellen, 1721), pp. 199–200.

79 *Thesouro Seraphico* (Coimbra, 1735), p. 95.

80 *Lezioni sopra la Regola dei Frati Minori di S. Francesco* (Venezia, 1753), p. 95.

81 *La Regola dé Frati Minori Esposta Praticamente* (Venezia, 1758), pp. 49-50; Gabriel-Angelo da Vicenza-Cosmas Sartori, *La Regola dei Frati Minori Esposta Praticamente* (Vicenza, 1937), pp. 107–108.

82 *Nuovo Manuale* (Venezia, 1758), p. 153.

83 *Dichiarazione Letterale, e Morale de' Precetti che si Contengono nella Regola de' Frati Minori* (Bologna, 1759), pp. 207–210.

84 *Liber Vitae* (Augustae Vindelicorum, 1761), p. 85; *Liber Vitae* (ad S. Mariae Angelorum prope Assisium, 1899), p. 75.

85 *Lo Spirito della Serafica Regola* (Brescia, 1761), p. 46.

Viatore da Coccaglio,[86] Christianus von Bienzheim,[87] Albertus a Bulsano,[88] Samuele Majocchi,[89] Georges de Villefranche,[90] Piatus Montensis,[91] Michael Sleutjes,[92] Zeno von Ufering,[93] Lizaso-Bolzano,[94] Nicholas of Cork [95] and Bede Hess.[96]

Even though the above listed authors make up the vast majority of the more important expositors of their time, a number of outstanding expositors, who deny the existence of a special precept of the Rule to fast before Easter, can be marshalled. Among them are: Girolamo Menghi,[97] Paolo Mondello,[98] Cyprianus Crousers,[99] Kazenberger-Iglesias,[100] Deodatus da Bivona [101] and Bernardino da Siena.[102]

Indisputably, the weight of the opinion of the commentators on

---

[86] *Tracce di Tradizione sopra la Regola de' Frati Minori* (Venezia, 1780), p. 81.

[87] *Kurze Unterweisungen ueber die Regel der Minder-Brueder* (Strasburgi, 1781), pp. 89–90.

[88] *Expositio Regulae FF. Minorum* (Oeniponte, 1850), § 43, n. 3; (Florentiae, 1864), § 43, n. 3; (Mediolani 1889), § 43, n. 3; (Romae, 1932), n. 167.

[89] *Esposizione Ascetico-Morale della Regola Minoritana* (Piacenza, 1856), p. 202.

[90] *Exposition de la Règle des Frères Mineurs* (Toulouse, 1893), p. 119.

[91] *Praelectiones Juris Regularis,* III, 38.

[92] *Commentarius in Constitutiones Generales Fratrum Minorum* (ad Claras Aquas, 1915), p. 270.

[93] *Erklaerung der Regel des heiligen seraphischen Vaters Franziskus* (Altoetting, 1929), p. 153.

[94] *Exposición de la Regla de los Frailes Menores* (Pamplona: PP. Capuchinos, 1939), p. 80.

[95] *Fast and Abstinence in Franciscan Legislation,* pp. 19–23.

[96] *Manuale de Regula et Constitutionibus Ordinis Fratrum Minorum Conventualium* (Romae: Typis Polyglottis Vaticanis, 1943), p. 92.

[97] *Giardino Delitioso de i Frati Minori* (Bologna, 1592), pp. 181–182.

[98] *Espositione sopra li xxvii. Praecetti della Regola di S. Francesco* (Napoli, 1608), pp. 249–250.

[99] *Lectiones Paraeneticae ad Regulam Seraphici Patris S. Francisci* (Coloniae Agrippinae, 1625), p. 168.

[100] *Liber Vitae* (ad Claras Aquas, 1926), p. 83; (Romae: Pontificium Athenaeum Antonianum, 1948), p. 107; (Romae, 1954), p. 103.

[101] *Esposizione Scolastica della Regola dei Frati Minori* (Palermo: Tip. "Fiamma Serafica," 1938), p. 64.

[102] *Esposizione della Regola Francescana,* n. 356; n. 371.

the Rule is overwhelmingly in favor of the existence of a special precept of the Rule to keep the Lent before Easter. There are modern authors who consider this concerted opinion of such great importance as to exclude the acceptableness of the opposite teaching.[103] But these writers fail to give proper consideration to the intrinsic arguments in the case. The authority of the past commentators on the Rule is of a merely private character. Their teaching is only as good as their arguments;[104] and it can be accepted only on that basis.

When they teach that the Rule proposes a special precept to keep the Lent before Easter, the commentators are not passing on a legal tradition of the Order. They are simply offering their own private interpretation of the Franciscan Rule. The point at issue is not tradition, nor is it custom. It is the interpretation of written law. If the commentators have been mistaken in what they taught, their teaching must be set aside. A glance at the principles of a few of the more outstanding of these commentators should make it quite evident that their conclusions cannot be accepted uncritically, and without a reexamination of their arguments.

Possibly the authority of no expositor of the Rule has been held in higher esteem than that of Antonius de Corduba (✝1578).[105] Surely, no one is more frequently cited for proof

[103] "Quae negantium sententia licet fundamento non spernendo fulciri videatur, eamdem tamen contra communem EE. doctrinam probare non ausim."—Sleutjes, *Commentarius in Constitutiones Generales Fratrum Minorum,* p. 270; "Hence from all the foregoing it is clear that the traditional interpretation considers Lent as a special precept of the Rule, and is so definite as to exclude the opposite opinion."—Nicholas of Cork, *Fast and Abstinence in Franciscan Legislation,* p. 23.

[104] "Interpretatio *doctrinalis,* cum fiat a personis privatis, maiorem vim obligatoriam non habet, quam ipsae rationes, quibus fulcitur."—Jone, *Commentarium in Codicem Iuris Canonici* (3 vols., Paderborn: Schoeningh, 1950–1955), I, 36.

[105] "Antonius Cordubensis, O.S. Franc. dum viveret, ut idoneus quidam atque ei aequalis testis loquitur, 'tamquam pythium quoddam erat theologiae oraculum, ad quem omnes auxilii et consilii gratia ventitabant . . .' "—Hurter, *Nomenclator Literarius Theologiae Catholicae* (5 vols., Vol. III, 3. ed., Oeniponte, 1907), p. 2.

that there is a special precept of the Rule regarding the Lent before Easter. Yet, in his commentary, he carefully and reservedly stated merely that "it seems more probable that they [the Franciscans] are bound also from the Rule." [106] Even so, his teaching is of questionable validity. He reached this conclusion in line with principles which today would meet with universal rejection. Seraphinus a Loiano calls him a "tutiorist." [107] Merkelbach considers him a probabiliorist.[108]

Santi Thesauro Romano, another expositor of great authority, employed the following wholly unacceptable argument to prove that the Rule incorporated a special precept to observe the Lent before Easter: "It is held to be true that the Rule does not explicitly use words of command; but it uses them implicitly, and given but not conceded that it did not use words of precept but of counsel; I say that words of counsel in grave and important matters are always preceptive." [109]

Filippo di Castellucio, a noted commentator of the eighteenth century, after he had affirmed, with some sense of uncertainty, that to him the more probable opinion seemed to be the one which taught the existence of a special precept of the Rule,[110] reached the startling conclusion that a Friar under twenty-one, who, as he taught, would be bound to the fasts of the Rule, would sin mortally if he violated that Lent.[111]

---

[106] "Probabilius videtur quod etiam ex regula tenentur."—*Expositio Evangelicae Regulae Seraphici Patris Sancti Francisci,* p. 152.

[107] *Institutiones Theologiae Moralis* (5 vols., Vol. I, Taurini: Marietti, 1934), n. 320.

[108] *Summa Theologiae Moralis* (3 vols., Vol. II, 8. ed., Parisiis: Desclée, 1949), p. 991.

[109] "Si risponde esser vero, che la Regola non usa esplicitamente parole di comandamento; ma le usa implicitamente, & dato sed non concesso, che non usasse parole di precetto, ma di conseglio; dico che le parole consultorie in materia grave, & importante sempre sono precettive."—*Espositione sopra la Regola del Serafico Padre S. Francesco,* p. 162.

[110] *Dichiarazione Letterale, e Morale de' Precetti che si Contengono nella Regola de' Frati Minori,* p. 209.

[111] "Epilogando dunque il discorso, dico, che, essendo questa non soltanto la più sicura, ma la più probabile, e comune sentenza, peccarebbe mortalmente quel Religioso, che non volesse osservare il digiuno della Quaresima, sotto pretesto di non esser giunto al terz settennio della sua età; perchè subito,

A study of some of the various editions of the *Liber Vitae* of Kilianus Kazenberger (✝1750) can be very instructive. It shows how the doctrine of this famous and venerable work came to be altered in accordance with the more accurate principles of the modern science of Canon Law. In the edition of 1761,[112] and even as late as the edition of 1899,[113] this commentary clearly taught that there exists a special precept of the Rule to observe the Lent which precedes Easter. The editions of 1926,[114] 1948 [115] and 1954,[116] however, all of which are edited by Antonius Iglesias teach that the obligation of this Lent arises solely from the common law.

The teachings of the older expositors of the Rule can be of the greatest value for every Franciscan when they concern the traditions and the spirit of the Order. But contemporary Friars cannot be held to every doctrinal interpretation of the Rule which they offer. The teaching of the expositors can and must be used to advantage wherever it is correct; but when it is in error, it must be rejected.

ARTICLE VI. THE FRIDAY FAST

The Friday fast, like the "Lent" before Christmas, was once obligatory for all Christians; but like this latter fast it also gradually lapsed into disuse.[117] Saint Francis restored its observance among his Friars by proposing an equivalent precept of the Rule: [118] "At other times they shall not be bound to fast except on Fridays." [119]

The expositors of the Rule discussed two thought-provoking

---

dopo la professione, è obbligato ai digiuni della Regola qualsivoglia Giovane." —*Dichiarazione Letterale, e Morale de' Precetti che si Contengono nella Regola de' Frati Minori*, p. 210.

112 See p. 85.

113 See p. 75.

114 See p. 83.

115 See p. 107.

116 See p. 103.

117 Wernz-Vidal, *Ius Canonicum*, IV, n. 520.

118 *Seraphicae Legislationis Textus Originales*, p. 237.

119 "Aliis autem temporibus non teneantur, nisi sexta feria ieiunare."—*Opuscula Sancti Patris Francisci*, p. 66.

questions that arose from the precept concerned with the Friday fast. The first dealt with the obligation of fasting if Christmas falls on a Friday. The second concerned the obligation of fasting on Fridays during the "Lent of Benediction."

Section 1. The Obligation to Fast When Christmas Falls on a Friday[120]

The Franciscan Rule is silent on the question of whether or not the Friday fast ceases when Christmas falls on that day. The commentators on the Rule have traditionally taught that the obligation does not cease, because: 1) the Rule makes no exception; and 2) general Church law obliges the Friars to follow the Rule and to fast when Christmas falls on a Friday. These two reasons are juridically complementary. Accordingly they must be treated together.

If Saint Francis had wished his Friars to be free from the obligation of fasting when Christmas falls on a Friday, he could easily have inserted a clause to that effect in the Rule. The Rule of the Second Order,[121] and also of the Third Order,[122] contains such a clause. The contemporary religious Rules of the Premonstratensians and the Dominicans, which prescribe the Friday fast, make similar provision for the cessation of that fast on Christmas.[123]

Whether Francis' failure to make such provision in the Rule of the First Order was intentional or not is uncertain. There is a temptation to believe that it was an oversight, because, in practice, Francis held that there was no fast when Christmas falls on a Friday.[124] Besides, the brevity and the general nature of the wording of the Rule argue against the inclusion of a prescription of such minor importance. But the reason for the omission is

---

[120] Fidel de Pamplona, "Ayunos y Abstinencias en la Regla Franciscana," *IS*, I (1955), 284–288.

[121] *Seraphicae Legislationis Textus Originales,* p. 56.

[122] *Seraphicae Legislationis Textus Originales,* p. 83.

[123] Fidel de Pamplona, "Ayunos y Abstinencias en la Regla Franciscana," *IS*, I. (1955), 285.

[124] Thomas de Celano, *Vita Secunda S. Francisci Assisiensis* (Ad Claras Aquas prope Florentiam, 1927), n. 199.

unimportant. The Rule must be understood as it was actually written, not as it might have been written.

Only an explicit exception in the Rule could have exempted the Friars from the law of fast when Christmas falls on a Friday, for, in the year 1222, Pope Honorius III had legislated that the members of the faithful were permited to eat meat if Christmas falls on a Friday, unless they were bound by a vow or by the regular observance. Twelve years later, Pope Gregory IX incorporated this enactment into the general law of the Church when he made it a part of his famous *Decretals*.[125] Since, at the time, abstinence from meat was considered to be part of the law of fast,[126] the exclusion of those who were bound by vow or by the regular observance from the permission to eat meat precluded any interpretation of the Franciscan Rule that would free the Friars from the obligation of fasting when Christmas fell on a Friday.

The obligation of fasting, therefore, did not arise from tradition, nor from custom, nor from the naked precept of the Rule. It arose from the precept of the Rule as it bound according to the disposition of Pope Honorius III. The expositors of the Rule have always interpreted it thus.[127]

---

125 "Honorius III. *Pragensi Episcopo.* Explicari per sedem apostolicam postulasti, *'utrum sit licitum illis, qui nec voto, nec regulari observantia sunt adstricti, carnes comedere, quando in sexta feria dies dominicae Nativitatis occurrit. Ad hoc'* Respondemus, quod illi, qui nec voto, nec regulari observantia sunt adstricti, in sexta feria, si festum nativitatis dominicae die ipso venire contigerit, carnibus propter festi excellentiam vesci possunt secundum consuetudinem ecclesiae generalis. Nec tamen hi reprehendendi sunt, qui ob devotionem voluerint abstinere." *Dat. Lat. IV. Kal. Nov. Pont. nostr. Ao. I.* (1216)—C. 3, X, *de observatione ieiuniorum,* III, 46.

126 Herrera, *Legislación Eclesiástica sobre el Ayuno y la Abstinencia,* pp. 70–71; S. Thomas Aquinas, *Summa Theologica* (Taurini: Marietti, 1905), IIa IIae, q. 147, a. 8.

127 Matthaeucci, *Schola Paupertatis* (Romae, 1731), p. 154; Bernardo da Bologna, *Lezioni sopra la Regola dei Frati Minori di S. Francesco,* p. 99; Gabriel-Angelo da Vicenza, *La Regola de' Frati Minori Esposta Praticamente, 1758,* p. 51; Kazenberger, *Liber Vitae, 1761,* p. 85; *1899,* p. 75; Kazenberger-Iglesias, *Liber Vitae, 1926,* p. 83; *1948,* p. 107; Filippo di Castellucio, *Dichiarazione Letterale, e Morale de' Precetti che si contengono nella Regola de' Frati Minori,* p. 216; Georges de Villefranche, *Exposition de la Règle des Frères Mineurs,* p. 121; Piatus Montensis, *Praelectiones*

If Pope Honorius had not excepted from his general ruling those who were bound by vow or by the regular observance, or if Pope Gregory had not incorporated his predecessor's legislation into his own authentic collection of decretals, the Friars would not have been obliged to fast when Christmas fell on a Friday. The Franciscan Rule, for example, unlike the contemporary religious Rules of the Poor Clares, of the Dominicans, and of the Premonstratensians,[128] did not make any exceptions in favor of the Sundays occurring during the Lents which it mentioned. Yet, the Friars have always considered themselves free from the obligation of fasting on those days.[129] They understood the obligation of the fast to cease on Sundays according to the norms of general Church law.

Several authors speak of an oral concession by which Pope Paul IV (1555–1559) granted permission to the Franciscans to eat meat whenever Christmas fell on a Friday.[130] Whatever may have been the worth of this concession, it does not seem to have met with general acceptance in practice.

The *Constitutiones Urbanae,* confirmed by Pope Urban VIII in the year 1628, ordained that the Friars Minor Conventual were not obliged to fast when Christmas fell on a Friday,[131] a prescription which is still retained in their present Constitutions.[132] In the

---

Juris Regularis, III, 39; Petrus Mocchegiani, *Iurisprudentia Ecclesiastica* (3 vols., ad Claras Aquas, 1904–1905), II, n. 85; Sleutjes, *Commentarius in Constitutiones Generales Fratrum Minorum,* p. 269; Fidel de Pamplona, "Ayunos y Abstinencias en la Regla Franciscana," *IS,* I (1955), 284.

128 Fidel de Pamplona, "Ayunos y Abstinencias en la Regla Franciscana," *IS,* I (1955), 285.

129 Fidel de Pamplona, "Ayunos y Abstinencias en la Regla Franciscana," *IS,* I (1955), 285.

130 Sanctorus de Melfi, *Morales Commentarii in Statuta, & Constitutiones Ordinis Fratrum Minorum S. P. N. Francisci de Observantia* (Romae, 1643), p. 335; Filippo di Castellucio, *Dichiarazione Letterale, e Morale de' Precetti che si Contengono nella Regola de' Frati Minori,* p. 216; Piatus Montensis, *Praelectiones Juris Regularis,* II, 38.

131 *Constitutiones Urbanae Ordinis Fratrum Minorum S. Francisci Conventualium* (Assisii, 1803), c. 3, n. 1.

132 *Constitutiones Ordinis Fratrum Minorum Sancti Patris Francisci Conventualium, 1932,* n. 318.

year 1953, the *Constitutiones Generales Ordinis Fratrum Minorum* made similar provision for the Order of Friars Minor.[133]

In neither of these cases do the respective Constitutions contain a dispensation from the Rule. There is no dispensation granted in favor of the Order of Friars Minor, inasmuch as the members of this branch of the Order are obliged to the pure and simple observance of the Rule.[134] There is no dispensation from the Rule granted in favor of the Order of Friars Minor Conventual, for before the promulgation of the Code of Canon Law, when this concession was first incorporated into the *Constitutiones Urbanae,* it had the effect of dispensing from the legislation of Pope Honorius III, but not from the Rule. As they stand today, the dispositions of both Constitutions merely declare the meaning of the Rule in view of the contemporary common law, each for its own branch of the Order.

Although their Constitutions do not treat of the question, the Friars Minor Capuchin too are free from the obligation of fasting whenever Christmas falls on a Friday. Before the promulgation of the Code, the Friars' obligation of fasting when Christmas fell on a Friday stemmed from an application of the Rule which had been imposed by the older law. The law has since changed. The Code of Canon Law has completely revised the whole subject matter of fast as contained in the former legislation; and thus it has superseded the older law.[135] Included in this changed order is the abrogation also of the ancient decretal of Pope Honorius III, which was so fundamental to the question of fasting in the Order whenever Christmas fell on a Friday. Whereas formerly the precept of the Rule had to be understood in accordance with that decretal, today it must be understood according to the law of the Code.

Canon 1253 states that, in the matter of fasting, the Code makes no changes in the Rules and Constitutions of any religious Institute. But since the Franciscan Rule contains no legislation on the precise problem under consideration, it is not affected by the ruling

[133] Art. 181, § 2, n. 2.

[134] *Constitutiones Generales Ordinis Fratrum Minorum, 1953,* art. 1.

[135] Canon 6.

contained in the canon. There is nothing in the Rule that leaves room for a change.

The legislation of the Franciscan Rule seeks simply to establish certain fast days. It provides none of the supplementary norms according to which the law of the fast must be observed. It depends upon the common law for such norms.[136]

The norm of the common law concerning fasting on a holy day of obligation is found in canon 1252, where it is stated that the law of fast ceases to bind on a holy day of obligation outside Lent. In keeping with this norm, the Friday fast of the Rule will cease for the Friars Minor Capuchin whenever Christmas happens to fall on a Friday.

An apparent difficulty is found in the answer given by the Sacred Congregation of Religious to a question put to it by the General Definitory of the Order of Friars Minor in the year 1921.[137] In this response, the Sacred Congregation declares that fasts prescribed by the Franciscan Rule do not cease on a holy day of obligation outside Lent. However, the response was directed only to the Procurator General of the Order of Friars Minor. It was not communicated to the Procurators General of the other two branches of the Order. Even though it is an authentic interpretation of the Rule, it is of a specific, and not of a generic character; and so it is binding only on the Order of Friars Minor.[138] It does not touch the members of the Order of Friars Minor Capuchin, who are free to take advantage of the concessions of the common law.

Section 2. The Friday Fast During the "Lent of Benediction"

After signalizing its dispositions with regard to the "Lent" before Christmas, and the Lent before Easter, the Franciscan Rule

---

136 Fidel de Pamplona, "Ayunos y Abstinencias en la Regula Franciscana," *IS*, I (1955), p. 287.

137 "Haec S. Congregatio, mature perpenso dubio exposito 'Utrum diebus festis de praecepto extra Quadragesimam cesset lex ieiunii, quae continetur in Regula Fratrum Minorum,' atque attentis omnibus ad rem facientibus, rescribendum censuit prout rescribit: 'Negative.' "—*Acta Ordinis Fratrum Minorum*, XL (1921), 125.

138 Canon 17, § 3.

continues: "But with regard to the Lent which begins at the Epiphany and lasts during the forty days which our Lord consecrated by His own fast, let those who keep it voluntarily be blessed by the Lord. . . . At other times they shall not be bound to fast except on Fridays." [139]

The phrase *at other times* in the listed quotation from the Rule has led some to question the obligation of fasting on the Fridays during the "Lent of Benediction." They reason as follows: The Rule enumerates three "Lents," two of which are obligatory, the other facultative. It then states that at times other than during the three "Lents" the Friars are not bound to fast except on Fridays. The phrase *at other times* restricts the special obligation of the Friday fast to those Fridays which fall outside any of the three "Lents." The obligation to fast on Friday, therefore, does not apply to the Fridays during the "Lent of Benediction." And since the "Lent of Benediction" is facultative, there is no obligation from any source to fast on a Friday during that "Lent." [140]

The foregoing interpretation of the Rule errs by considering merely the grammatical context in which the phrase is found. It completely ignores the purpose of the passage. The idea that the Rule wishes to convey is this: At times other than when they are observing a "Lent" the Friars are bound to fast only on Friday. If a Friar observes all three "Lents," he need otherwise fast only on the remaining Fridays of the year. If he observes only the two obligatory "Lents," he similarly needs to fast only on the remaining Fridays of the year. But in this latter case he will be bound to fast also on those Fridays which fall within the "Lent of Benediction."

Pope Clement V would not have stated so absolutely in the *Exivi* that an equivalent precept of the Rule obliged the Friars to

---

139 "Sanctam vero quadragesimam, quae incipit ab Epiphania usque ad continuos quadraginta dies, quam Dominus suo sancto ieiunio consecravit, qui voluntarie eam ieiunant, benedicti sint a Domino . . . Aliis autem temporibus non teneantur, nisi sexta feria, ieiunare."—*Opuscula Sancti Patris Francisci,* p. 66.

140 Cf. Marchant, *Expositio Literalis in Regulam S. Francisci,* pp. 170–172; Matthaeucci, *Schola Paupertatis,* pp. 154–156.

fast on Fridays[141] if the Rule had intended to except all the Fridays during the "Lent of Benediction." Nor would the Pope have used the phrase *at other times*[142] only in reference to the "Lents" before Christmas and Easter if the Rule had intended that it should apply also to the "Lent of Benediction" in such a manner as to remove the obligation of the Friday fast.[143]

Notwithstanding the grammatical difficulties involved, the question of fasting on the Fridays that occur during the "Lent of Benediction" has never posed a problem to the expositors of the Rule. The great majority do not even discuss it. Their silence shows quite simply that they saw no difficulty. The general meaning of the passage was clear to them, despite the grammatical deficiencies in the manner of its expression.

Article VII. The "Lent of Benediction"

Unlike the other "Lents" which it mentions, the Seraphic Rule does not impose under obligation the "Lent" following the Feast of the Epiphany. The Rule states: "But with regard to the Lent which begins at the Epiphany and lasts during the forty days which our Lord consecrated by His own fast, let those who keep it voluntarily be blessed by the Lord; but those who do not wish to keep it shall not be obliged."[144] The observance of this "Lent" is left entirely to the individual Friar's zeal for perfection. Saint Francis furnished the Friars two motives in the Rule as an incentive to observe the "Lent": 1) the example of our divine Savior; and 2) God's special blessing to be bestowed on those who fast. Hence the name by which it is known, the "Lent of Benediction."

---

141 ". . . item, quod *ieiunare . . . in sextis feriis teneantur."—Seraphicae Legislationis Textus Originales,* p. 237.

142 "Aliis autem temporibus."

143 ". . . cum duobus temporibus annotatis in Regula, scilicet *a festo omnium Sanctorum usque ad Nativitatem Domini, et* maximae Quadragesimae, in quibus ieiunare tenentur, inseratur in eadem Regula: *Aliis autem temporibus non teneantur nisi sexta feria ieiunare."—Seraphicae Legislationis Textus Originales,* p. 242.

144 "Sanctam vero quadragesimam, quae incipit ab Epiphania usque ad continuos quadraginta dies, quam Dominus suo sancto ieiunio consecravit, qui voluntarie eam ieiunant, benedicti sint a Domino, et qui nolunt, non sint adstricti."—*Opuscula Sancti Patris Francisci,* p. 66.

In the *Regula Prima,* Saint Francis imposed the "Lent of Benediction" under precept, as part of a fast extending from the Feast of the Epiphany until Easter;[145] but in the *Regula Bullata,* without commanding it, he merely urged the Friars to observe that "Lent" as a special work of love. Love for God, not legal compulsion, was to effect its observance in the Order.

Saint Bonaventure called the "Lent of Benediction" a fast of joy, for the Friars observed it in commemoration of and in imitation of Christ's own fast. During the "Lent of Benediction," so wrote the Seraphic Doctor, "a zealous Franciscan's heart is so filled with spiritual delights that it actually becomes a penance for him to partake of material food. He observes the 'Lent' joyfully, for he looks upon it not so much as a mortification as a means toward preserving devotion; and devotion is the Franciscan soul's greatest delight."[146]

The Gospels narrate that after his baptism Christ went forth into the desert, where he fasted forty days and forty nights.[147] Franciscans imitate this fast when they observe the "Lent of Benediction." Therefore they begin the "Lent" with the Epiphany, which, until the year 1956, was the feast which commemorated Christ's baptism,[148] and they keep it during the next forty days, which our Lord consecrated by his own fast.

In actual practice, however, out of reverence for the solemnity of the feast, the Friars have customarily begun to fast, not on the feast day itself, but on the following day, January 7.[149] Strictly

145 "Et similiter omnes fratres ieiunent . . . ab Epiphania, quando Dominus noster Iesus Christus incepit ieiunare, usque ad Pascha."—*Opuscula Sancti Patris Francisci,* p. 29.

146 "Ieiunium vero *gaudii* est, cum ipsum cor tantis est inunctum spiritualibus deliciis, ut poena sit ei vacare mensis; et est per consequens delectabile ieiunare, cum ieiunatur, non ut corpus affligatur, sed ne devotio interrumpatur, qua spiritus recreatur . . . Ieiunium autem Christi significat ieiunium *gaudii,* quo non tantum a cibis, sed ab omnibus terrenis delectationibus abstinetur."—"Expositio super Regulam Fratrum Minorum," *Opera Omnia,* VIII, 409.

147 Matth., 3:13–17; 4:1–11; Mark, 1:9–13; Luke, 3:21–22; 4:1–13.

148 "Decretum Generale de Rubricis ad Simpliciorem Formam Redigendis," *Acta Apostolicae Sedis,* XLVII (1955), 220–221.

149 Santi Thesauro Romano, *Espositione sopra la Regola del Seráfico Padre S. Francesco,* p. 174; Bernardo da Bologna, *Lezioni sopra la Regola dei Frati Minori di S. Francesco,* p. 97.

taken, therefore, since they fast only until February 14 inclusively, according to the custom of many provinces,[150] the Friars of those provinces do not observe a full "Lent" of forty days. If the number of actual days of fast is considered, the "Lent" is still shorter, for the Friars conform themselves to the universal practice of all Christians in not fasting on Sundays.

As it is actually observed, therefore, the "Lent of Benediction" will never perfectly correspond to the fast of Christ in the sense that it comprises forty uninterrupted days of fast. But that is not its purpose. It is supposed to be a sanctification of the time which Christ devoted to fasting, not a perfect imitation of the fast itself. For the same reason, it is meaningless to postpone the close of the "Lent of Benediction" until February 15 inclusively, for the reason that its opening has already been postponed from January 6 to January 7. After February 14, the period consecrated by Christ's fast is over. Any further days of fast simply cannot be part of the "Lent of Benediction."

Similarly, one who undertakes to fast for only a part of that forty-day period performs a meritorious work, but he does not observe the "Lent of Benediction," nor does he partake of the special blessing given to the Friars who keep it in its entirety.[151] Nevertheless, those who are unable to observe the "Lent" must not be considered as excluded from the graces and divine protection merited for the community as such by those who fast.[152]

The "Lent of Benediction" is one of the so-called "liberties" of the Rule, but it is not a liberty in any absolute sense. A Superior, for example, can forbid a Friar to fast if he sees that fasting will be detrimental to his health or to his spiritual well-being.[153]

Contrariwise, however, a Superior cannot command an unwilling Friar to fast.[154] To inject the idea of obligation from whatever

---

150 *Caeremoniale Romano-Seraphicum ad Usum Ordinis Fratrum Minorum Capuccinorum,* Romae: apud Curiam Generalem O.F.M. Cap., 1944, n. 2201.

151 Bernardo da Bologna, *Lezioni sopra la Regola dei Frati Minori di S. Francesco,* p. 97.

152 Sleutjes, *Commentarius in Constitutiones Generales Fratrum Minorum,* p. 275.

153 Gabriel-Angelo da Vicenza-Cosmas Sartori, *La Regola dei Frati Minori,* p. 107.

154 Albertus a Bulsano, *Expositio Regulae FF. Minorum, 1932,* n. 166.

source into the "Lent of Benediction" is to change its whole character. The Rule urges the Friars to observe the "Lent" in imitation of Christ and in commemoration of his fast; and it promises a blessing to those who keep the "Lent" voluntarily. These two elements constitute the very essence of the "Lent of Benediction" as it stands in the Rule. They both demand a free choice on the part of the Friars; and they are both incompatible with compulsion. They exclude the very possibility of a Superior's commanding a friar to observe the "Lent of Benediction." [155] The final words of the Rule on the subject are: "Those who do not wish to keep it shall not be obliged." [156] They thus conclusively rule out any idea of obligation.

Although Superiors cannot compel the unwilling to observe the "Lent of Benediction," they need not, on the other hand, provide special food for them. Rather, they should encourage the observance of the "Lent of Benediction" among their subjects by serving Lenten fare in accordance with the needs of those who are fasting, while at the same time providing a sufficient quantity, so that those who do not wish to fast are not compelled to do so.[157]

Article VIII. The Subject of the Fast

Section 1. The Former Teaching

The expositors of the Franciscan Rule who wrote during the centuries before the promulgation of the Code of Canon Law were in almost unanimous agreement when they discussed the subject

155 "Ad quadragesimam, quae incipit ab epiphania, quam vocamus benedictam, nullo modo compellantur fratres ieiunare, cum hoc diametraliter repugnet regulae."—*Constitutiones Salmantacenses, 1553* (Romae, 1576), p. 15; *Constitutiones Romanae, 1642* (Romae, 1642), c. 5, n. 5; "Constitutiones Vallisoletanae, 1593," De Gubernatis, *Orbis Seraphicus,* III, 440–441; *Constitutiones Capistranae, 1768* (Romae, 1827), n. 224; *Constitutiones Generales Ordinis Fratrum Minorum, 1953,* art. 186.

156 "Et qui nolunt, non sint adstricti."—*Opuscula Sancti Patris Francisci,* p. 66.

157 *Ordinationes Capitulorum Generalium Ordinis Minorum Capuccinorum* (Romae, 1928), Ord. 77; Bernardino da Siena, *Esposizione della Regola Francescana,* n. 373; Albertus a Bulsano, *Expositio Regulae FF. Minorum, 1932,* n. 166.

of fast in the Order.[158] When speaking of fasts which were imposed by the common law alone, they taught that the Friars were bound in exactly the same way as the rest of the faithful, since the law bound them not precisely as Franciscans, but simply as members of the faithful. Therefore, they concluded, only those Friars who were older than twenty-one and younger than fifty-nine were obliged to these fasts.[159]

On the other hand, when speaking of fasts that were imposed

---

[158] Anonymous, *Esposizione della Regola de' Frati Minori di S. Francesco* (Firenze, 1594), p. 152; Mondello, *Espositione sopra li xxvii. Precetti della Regola di S. Francesco,* p. 251; Hieronymus a Politio, *Expositio,* pp. 291–292; Antonius M. de Corduba, *Expositio Evangelicae Regulae Seraphici Patris Sancti Francisci,* p. 152; Santi Thesauro Romano, *Espositione sopra la Regola del Seráfico Padre S. Francesco,* p. 173; Rodericus, *Quaestiones Regulares et Canonicae,* II, 297–298; Antonio da Patti, *Considerationi et Espositioni sopra Tutti li Precetti della Regola de' Frati Minori,* p. 244; Crousers, *Lectiones Paraeneticae ad Regulam Seraphici Patris S. Francisci,* p. 190; Giovanni Battista da Monza, *Espiacatione della Regola di San Francesco,* p. 228; Bruno Chassaing, *Sanctus Franciscus Redivivus* (Parisiis, 1652), p. 37; Bona-Gratia Habsensis, *Compendiosa Summula Selectarum Quaestionum Regularium,* n. 217; Anonymous, *Doctrina para Criar los Novicios de la Orden de Nuestro Padre San Francisco* (Valladolid, 1718), pp. 120–121; Bernardinus von Gend, *Ausslegung ueber die Regel der Minderbrueder,* p. 194; Matthaeucci, *Schola Paupertatis,* p. 156; Valerio do Sacramento, *Thesouro Seraphico,* p. 93; pp. 96–99; Bernardo da Bologna, *Lezioni sopra la Regola dei Frati Minori di S. Francesco,* p. 95; Gabriel-Angelo da Vicenza, *La Regola de' Frati Minori Esposta Praticamente,* pp. 52–53; Filippo di Castellucio, *Dichiarazione Letterale, e Morale de' Precetti che si Contengono nella Regola de' Frati Minori,* pp. 177–183; Kilianus Kazenberger, *Liber Vitae, 1761,* pp. 91–92; *1899,* pp. 80–81; Gaudenzio da Brescia, *Lo Spirito della Serafica Regola,* p. 46; Christianus von Bienzheim, *Kurze Unterweisungen ueber die Regel der Minder-Brueder,* p. 87; Viatore da Coccaglio, *Tracce di Tradizione sopra la Regola de' Frati Minori,* pp. 87–88; Albertus a Bulsano, *Expositio Regulae FF. Minorum, 1850,* § 45, n. 1; *1864,* § 45, n. 1; *1889,* § 45, n. 1; Majocchi, *Esposizione Ascetico-Morale della Regola Minoritana,* p. 202; Georges de Villefranche, *Exposition de la Règle des Frères Mineurs,* pp. 122–123; Piatus Montensis, *Praelectiones Juris Regularis,* III, 40; Mocchegiani, *Iurisprudentia Ecclesiastica,* II, n. 82; Eugenio da Pontremoli, *Breve Esposizione della Regola Minoritana* (Firenze, 1911), pp. 44–45.

[159] Herrera, *Legislación Eclesiástica sobre el Ayuno y la Abstinencia,* p. 159.

only by the law of the Order, or of those which were simultaneously imposed by the law of the Order and by the common law, they presented a variant doctrine. They reasoned that, when he made profession, a Franciscan bound himself freely and unreservedly to the full observance of the Rule. Neither the Rule nor the profession which he made allowed for the exemption of any Friar from the obligation of fast simply in consideration of his age. Therefore, they held, every Friar was bound to observe these fasts from the moment of his profession until death.

Although no professed Friar could, in the strict sense of the term, be regarded as exempt from the obligation of fasting as imposed by the Rule, the expositors commonly considered sexagenarians as excused, under the heading that old age is equivalent to sickness. If the excusing cause was not clearly manifest, they taught that Superiors could dispense with a safe conscience. Only in rare instances did they consider an exceptionally robust aged friar as bound to fast.[160]

The expositors were not so indulgent towards those who were under twenty-one. They were generally agreed that youth, of itself, was not an excusing cause. It is strange that they should have failed to recognize that the underdevelopment of normal health and strength, which is characteristic of youth, is very similar to the ebbing of this normal health and strength in the aged. If they recognized old age as an excusing cause, they should likewise have recognized youth as an excusing cause.[161]

Section 2. The Present Teaching

In recent decades a more benign spirit has made itself felt in ecclesiastical legislation. One of its effects among the Franciscans has been to bring about a change in the teaching of the expositors of the Rule regarding the subject of the fasts of the Rule. At one

---

160 "Ma il Navarro non ammette queste ragioni, perche parlando di se stesso dice c'havendo 80. anni, poteva digiunare commodamente, come faceva ne' 50. Però Questo si rimette al giuditio del Prelato, quando il Frate per vecchiezza sia scusato."—Santi Thesauro Romano, *Espositione sopra la Regola del Seráfico Padre S. Francesco,* p. 175.

161 Sleutjes, *Commentarius in Constitutiones Generales Fratrum Minorum,* p. 272.

time the expositors looked upon the determination of the subject of these fasts as a very special problem. Today they teach that that subject is determined in exactly the same way as the subject of any Church fast.[162] The underlying reason for the present teaching rests upon a more careful consideration of the juridic consequences of religious profession in the Order.

When a Franciscan makes profession, he uses these words:

> I, Brother N. N., vow and promise to Almighty God, to the Blessed Virgin Mary, to our Holy Father Saint Francis, and to all the Saints, and to you, Father, to observe (*for three years—until I have completed my twenty-first year—all the days of my life*) the Rule of the Friars Minor, confirmed by our Lord Pope Honorius, living in obedience, without property, and in chastity.[163]

According to the foregoing formula of profession, a Franciscan vows and promises to observe the Rule. But that does not mean that he obliges himself under vow to observe everything prescribed by the Rule. Saint Thomas Aquinas taught the following: "He who professes the Rule does not vow to observe everything contained in the Rule; but he vows the regular life, which consists

---

[162] Sleutjes, *Commentarius in Constitutiones Generales Fratrum Minorum,* pp. 271–273; Kazenberger-Iglesias, *Liber Vitae, 1926,* pp. 90–91; *1948,* pp. 115–116; *1954,* pp. 112–113; Zeno von Ufering, *Erklaerung der Regel des heiligen Seraphischen Vaters Franziskus,* pp. 155–156; Albertus a Bulsano, *Expositio Regulae FF. Minorum, 1932,* n. 181; Lizaso-Bolzano, *Exposición de la Regla de los Frailes Menores,* p. 85; Gabriel-Angelo da Vicenza-Cosmas Sartori, *La Regola dei Frati Minori Esposta Praticamente,* pp. 110–112; Anonymous, *Quaestiones Quaedam de Ieiunio et Abstinentia in Ordine Fratrum Minorum* (Romae: apud Curiam Generalem Ordinis FF. Min. Cap., 1942), p. 18; Isidorus Trienekens, *Expositio Canonico-Moralis Regulae Fratrum Minorum* (4. ed., Mechliniae: Typographia S. Francisci, 1948), nn. 218–222; Bernardino da Siena, *Esposizione della Regola Francescana,* n. 358; Goyeneche, *Quaestiones Canonicae de Iure Religiosorum,* II, 345–349.

[163] "Ego Frater N. a N. voveo et promitto Deo omnipotenti, beatae Mariae Virgini, beato Patri nostro Francisco, omnibus Sanctis, et tibi, Pater (ad triennium—usque ad vigesimum primum aetatis annum expletum—toto tempore vitae meae) servare Regulam Fratrum Minorum, per Dominum Papam Honorium confirmatam, vivendo in obedientia, sine proprio, et in castitate."—*Caeremoniale Romano-Seraphicum ad Usum Ordinis Fratrum Minorum Capuccinorum,* n. 2820.

essentially in the three (vows)."[164] From these words of the Angelic Doctor, it is evident that, even though the Friar makes the Rule the object of his profession, a Franciscan obliges himself under vow only to the observance of the three essential evangelical counsels of the religious life.

Nevertheless, when he makes profession, a Franciscan takes on other obligations in addition to and distinct from the naked observance of the three vows.[165] These are the precepts of the Rule. When he explained the nature of the obligation of these precepts in the decretal *Exivi,* Pope Clement V very precisely distinguished between them and the vows, at the same time affirming that they were of strict obligation.[166]

The precepts of the Rule bind, not as vows, but as precepts of law.[167] They are part of the fundamental law,[168] the Franciscan Rule, which the Holy See has approved for the governing of the Order. When a Franciscan makes profession, he enters the Order, and, while he does not vow the Rule, he nevertheless subjects himself to it and to all the obligations which it imposes as to a law which he must observe.

In the matter of fast, the Rule demands much more of Franciscans than the common law demands of the faithful in general. But it does not make this demand in a manner that is completely divorced from the common law. When the Rule commands fasting, it commands it as fasting is understood according to the common law.[169]

---

164 "Ille qui profitetur regulam, non vovet servare omnia quae sunt in regula; sed vovet regularem vitam, quae essentialiter consistit in tribus praedictis."—*Summa Theologica,* IIa IIae, q. 186, a. 9, ad 1.

165 *Seraphicae Legislationis Textus Originales,* p. 234.

166 *Seraphicae Legislationis Textus Originales,* pp. 234–235.

167 Sleutjes, *Commentarius in Constitutiones Generales Fratrum Minorum,* p. 272; Victorius ab Appeltern, *Dissertatio de Modo Quo Diversa Ieiunia et Abstinentiae a Religiosis Familiis Hodiendum sunt Observanda* (Romae, 1917), p. 9; Kazenberger-Iglesias, *Liber Vitae, 1926,* p. 90; *1948,* p. 115; *1954,* p. 112; Trienekens, *Expositio Canonico-Moralis Regulae Fratrum Minorum,* n. 222.

168 Cf. Wernz-Vidal, *Ius Canonicum* (7 vols., Vol. III, Romae: Apud Aedes Universitatis Gregorianae, 1933), n. 368, I.

169 Fidel de Pamplona, "Ayunos y Abstinencias en la Regla Franciscana," *IS,* I (1955), 285.

Thus, unless some other provision is made by legitimate authority, all the supplementary norms of the common law which determine the nature of fasting in the concrete are to be applied to the fasts proposed in the Rule. Among these norms is that which states that only those who are between the ages of twenty-one and fifty-nine are bound to fast.[170] Since the Rule makes no provision to the contrary, Franciscans may follow this norm with regard to the fasts proposed in the Rule, with the exception of the Friars Minor Conventual, who by their Constitutions are bound, no matter of what age they may be, to observe the fasts proposed in the Rule.[171]

From what has been said, it cannot be concluded that the Rule imposes unequal obligations on different friars simply on the score of a difference in physical age. An inequality does exist; but that inequality arises not from the Rule, but from the common law.

Section 3. A Parallel Case

There is found in the Rule another case in which, like the case of fasting, Franciscans are apparently held to unequal obligations from their profession. The Rule commands the Friars to recite the Divine Office according to the use of the Roman Church.[172] Yet those Friars alone who have made profession of solemn vows are obliged to recite the Office privately if they have been absent from the choral recitation, while those who have made profession of simple vows are under no such obligation. Still, except for the length of time for which each takes his vows, a simply professed Friar and a solemnly professed Friar promise exactly the same thing at profession. The inequality of the obligation incumbent upon each stems neither from the Rule nor from their respective professions. It arises solely from the extrinsic disposition of the common law.[173]

The two cases are closely parallel. In precisely the same manner

---

[170] Canon 1254, § 2.

[171] *Constitutiones Ordinis Fratrum Minorum Sancti Patris Francisci Conventualium, 1932,* n. 323.

[172] "Clerici faciant divinum officium secundum ordinem sanctae Romanae Ecclesiae."—*Opuscula Sancti Patris Francisci,* p. 66.

[173] Canon 610, § 3.

as the common law imposes these unequal obligations upon different Friars with regard to the recitation of the Divine Office by reason of profession, so too does that same common law impose unequal obligations on different Friars with regard to the observance of the fasts proposed in the Rule by reason of age.

ARTICLE IX. FURTHER PRESCRIPTIONS

Before the time of Pope Clement V (1305–1314) [174] there seems to have been a great deal of discussion concerning the phrase found in the third chapter of the Franciscan Rule, which reads: "At other times they shall not be bound to fast." [175] Fixing their attention too much on the mere wording of the Rule, some of the ancient expositors maintained that Franciscan Friars were exempt from all fasts except those proposed in the Rule of their Order.

If this teaching possessed any probability previous to his time, Pope Clement put an end to it. In the decretal *Exivi,* he issued a clear and precise interpretation of the clause.[176] He stated that the words mean merely that the Friars are not bound to fast at times other than during the fasts prescribed by the Church. To clear up all doubt, he added that neither the author of the Rule nor the Pope who confirmed it could have had any intention to dispense the Friars from the fasts which are of obligation for other Christians.

The phrase is simply a negative general conclusion to the Rule's treatise on fasting. After he indicated positively the fasts to which the Friars are obliged by the Rule, Saint Francis rounded out the picture by stating that the Friars shall be bound to no other fasts in virtue of the Rule.

ARTICLE X. EXCUSING CAUSES

Saint Francis concluded his discussion on fasting as proposed in

---

[174] Cf. *Seraphicae Legislationis Textus Originales,* p. 242.

[175] "Aliis autem temporibus non teneantur . . . ieiunare."—*Opuscula Sancti Patris Francisci,* p. 66.

[176] "Declaramus debere intelligi eos non teneri ad ieiunium temporibus, praeterquam in ieiuniis ab Ecclesia institutis. Non enim est verisimile quod vel institutor Regulae vel etiam confirmator absolvere eos intenderit a servandis illis ieiuniis ad quae de communi statuto Ecclesiae obligantur ceteri Christiani."—*Seraphicae Legislationis Textus Originales,* pp. 242–243.

the Rule by stating: "In cases, however, of manifest necessity, the Friars are not obliged to observe corporal fasts." [177]

The Saint here enunciated the principle that his Friars were to follow in determining the existence of causes that would excuse them from the obligation of fasting. The principle is simple and direct. Yet, like so much of the Franciscan Rule, the concise manner in which the principle is stated, as also the general manner in which it is expressed, has led to a great deal of controversy among the expositors of the Rule concerning its meaning.

Some have taught that the principle demands a greater necessity as an excuse from a Rule fast than is required as an excuse from the common law fast.[178] Others have taught that a lesser necessity suffices.[179] Still others, and these by far constitute the majority, have taught that any necessity that excuses from a purely common law fast excuses also from a Rule fast.[180]

The use of the word *manifest* as employed in the Rule has been the chief source of difficulty. Some of the commentators on the Rule were of the opinion that a *manifest necessity* is something more than the common necessity that excuses from ecclesiastical

---

[177] "Tempore vero manifestae necessitatis non teneantur fratres ieiunio corporali."—*Opuscula Sancti Patris Francisci,* p. 66.

[178] Marchant, *Expositio Literalis in Regulam S. Francisci,* p. 175; Matthaeucci, *Schola Paupertatis,* p. 157; Bernardinus von Gend, *Ausslegung ueber die Regel der Minderbrueder,* p. 207; Albertus a Bulsano, *Expositio Regulae FF. Minorum, 1850,* § 45; *1864,* § 45; *1889,* § 45.

[179] Cf. Piatus Montensis, *Praelectiones Juris Regularis,* III, 46.

[180] Sanctorus de Melfi, *Morales Commentarii in Statuta, & Constitutiones Ordinis Fratrum Minorum S. P. N. Francisci de Observantia,* p. 336; Chassaing, *Sanctus Franciscus Redivivus,* p. 37; Kazenberger, *Liber Vitae, 1761,* p. 93; *1899,* p. 81; Kazenberger-Iglesias, *Liber Vitae, 1926,* p. 90; *1948,* pp. 114–115; *1954,* p. 111; Christianus von Bienzheim, *Kurze Unterweisungen ueber die Regel der Minder-Brueder,* p. 93; Georges de Villefranche, *Exposition de la Règle des Frères Mineurs,* pp. 123–124; Eugenio da Pontremoli, *Breve Esposizione della Regola Minoritana,* p. 46; Sleutjes, *Commentarius in Constitutiones Generales Fratrum Minorum,* p. 273; Zeno von Ufering, *Erklaerung der Regel des heiligen Seraphischen Vaters Franziskus,* p. 156; Albertus a Bulsano, *Expositio Regulae FF. Minorum, 1932,* n. 180; Gabriel-Angelo da Vicenza-Cosmas Sartori, *La Regola dei Frati Minori Esposta Praticamente,* p. 120; Deodatus a Bivona, *Esposizione Scolastica della Regola dei Frati Minori,* p. 66; Trienekens, *Expositio Canonico-Moralis Regulae Fratrum Minorum,* n. 220.

fasts. The meaning of the word *manifest,* however, does not call for such an interpretation. To be manifest, a necessity need not be recognizable as such to everyone who encounters it. It is sufficient that it be recognizable to any properly qualified person who is called upon to judge.

Already in the early history of the Order, Hugo a Digna set down a safe and reasonable interpretation of the phrase in question.[181] He taught that a necessity is manifest whenever any intelligent and discreet person feels no doubt as to its actual existence, especially when that person happens to be a Superior. Although any prudent person is capable of judging on the presence of a manifest necessity, not excluding the party himself, it is always best for a subject to have recourse to his Superior, since a Superior can supply for any deficiency in the necessity by granting a dispensation.[182]

It is evident, therefore, that the norm as proposed in the Rule calls for no greater necessity as an excuse from a fast indicated in the Rule than is required as an excuse from a fast ordered by the Church. Since this is so, it follows that the various reasons which theologians advance as causes excusing from the Church fast will have application also to the fasts prescribed in the Franciscan Rule.

---

181 "Necessitas dicitur manifesta quando intelligenti vel discreto cuilibet, et maxime Praelato, dubia non existit."—"Expositio Fratris Hugonis super Regulam," Bonifatius a Ceva, *Speculum Minorum seu Firmamentum Trium Ordinum,* pars III, fol. 37.

182 Kazenberger-Iglesias, *Liber Vitae, 1954,* p. 110.

CHAPTER II

THE LEGISLATION OF THE CONSTITUTIONS

Introduction

Since the publication of the first Franciscan Constitutions, the *Constitutiones Narbonenses,* in the year 1260, the Order, in its various branches, has seen at least sixty-one different subsequent editions.[1] The primary rôle of the Constitutions with regard to fast and abstinence has been that of accommodating the legislation of the Rule and the traditions of the Order to the needs of the times. The dispositions which the Constitutions have implemented in their successive editions are indeed varied and many.

For the sake of making this study as simple as possible, the discussion regarding the several editions of the Constitutions will be arranged according to two principal articles. The first of these articles will treat the substantial part of the legislation of the Constitutions regarding fast and abstinence. It will treat primarily of the days of fast and the days of abstinence which they prescribe. The second article will treat of the elements incidental to that legislation. It will relate to every relevant enactment in the Constitutions that has not been treated in the first article.

Each of the two principal articles will, in turn, serve in successive sections to explain in order: 1) the early discipline of the Constitutions from the foundation of the Order until its division; 2) the discipline of the Constitutions of the Friars Minor Conventual; 3) the discipline of the Constitutions of the Friars Minor of the Observant families; and 4) the discipline of the Constitutions of the Friars Minor Capuchin.

[1] The arrangement of the Constitutions drawn up by Marinus a Neukirchen in the article, "Constitutionum Generalium Primi Ordinis Seraphici Series Chronologica," *Collectanea Franciscana,* XII (1942), 377–396, has been followed throughout this chapter. See also Marinus a Neukirchen, *De Capitulo Generali in Primo Ordine Seraphico,* pp. 508–526.

Article I. Prescribed Days of Fast and Abstinence

Section 1. The Early Constitutions

It was not long after the death of Saint Francis that the primitive simplicity of the legislation on fasting in the Franciscan Rule began to undergo successive modifications. The Rule itself was not changed, but the Constitutions of the Order incorporated further prescriptions to supplement the legislation of the Rule. In the very first *Constitutiones Generales* of the Order, published by the Chapter of Narbonne in 1260, the Fathers of the Chapter decreed that the vigils of the feasts of certain of the Apostles should be kept as days of fast.[2] The reason for this is not difficult to find. The faithful of the time were accustomed to fast on the vigils of the feasts of many of the Apostles, but there was no uniform practice as to which ones should be kept.[3] In a religious Institute as large as the Franciscan Order had then become,[4] it was necessary that some common discipline be adopted, regardless of the practice of the faithful at large. It is worthy of note that the Friars modeled their own legislation on the practice that was then current in Rome.[5] The Order learned well the lesson of love and reverence toward the Holy See which Saint Francis had taught by word and example. Besides the above mentioned vigils of the feasts of the Apostles, the Fathers of the Chapter also commanded that the vigil of the Feast of Saint Francis be kept as a day of fast.[6]

The dispositions of these first Constitutions remained unchanged in their various editions previous to the first division within the

---

[2] "Apostolorum vigiliae ieiunentur intus et extra, Beatorum Philippi et Iacobi et Iohannis Evangelistae et Barnabae tantum exceptis. Vigilia B. Bartholomaei ieiunetur et festum secundum morem patriae fiat. Vigilia B. Francisci ieiunetur."—"Constitutiones Narbonenses, 1260," *AFH,* XXXIV (1941), p. 55, n. 2.

[3] Herrera, *Legislación Eclesiástica sobre el Ayuno y la Abstinencia,* p. 57.

[4] ". . . numerus fratrum in toto ordine exsistentium versus finem saeculi XIII erit aestimandus ad 30,000—40,000."—Holzapfel, *Manuale Historiae Ordinis Fratrum Minorum,* p. 145.

[5] Herrera, *Legislación Eclesiástica sobre el Ayuno y la Abstinencia,* p. 57.

[6] "Constitutiones Narbonenses, 1260," *AFH,* XXXIV (1941), p. 55, n. 2.

Order.[7] Their wording is repeated even in Constitutions of the Ultramontane Observants after the division.[8]

Section 2. The Constitutions of the Friars Minor Conventual

The first Constitutions of the Conventual Franciscans which were generally accepted and put into practice,[9] the *Constitutiones Alexandrinae* of 1500, stated, with regard to days of fast and abstinence, that the Friars were bound to the same fasts as other Christians, in addition to the obligation of fasting on the vigil of the Feast of Saint Francis.[10] At first glance, such a disposition could seem like a relaxation of the older discipline. Actually it was merely a simplification, for, with the exception of the fasts stemming from the Franciscan Rule and the fast on the vigil of the Feast of Saint Francis, the faithful of that time were observing as fast days all the vigils to which the Friars had been bound by the earlier Constitutions. In fact, they were observing more, for before the end of the fourteenth century it had also become the common practice to fast on the vigils of the Feasts of Saint John the Baptist, Saint Lawrence, and All Saints.[11] Since they were in no way exempt from the common obligations of the faithful in the matter of fast, the Friars too were keeping these vigils as days of fast.

[7] "Constitutiones Assisienses, 1279," *AFH,* XXXIV (1941), p. 59, n. 2; "Constitutiones Parisienses, 1292," *AFH,* XXXIV (1941), p. 59, n. 2; "Constitutiones Assisienses, 1316," *AFH,* IV (1911), p. 282, n. 2; "Statuta Caturcensia, 1337," *AFH,* XXX (1937), p. 132, n. 2; "Constitutiones Assisienses, 1340," *AFH,* VI (1913), p. 259, n. 2; "Statuta Lugdunensia, 1351," *AFH,* XXX (1937), p. 163, n. 2; "Constitutiones Farineriae, 1354," *AFH,* XXXV (1942), p. 97, n. 2.

[8] "Constitutiones Barcinonenses, 1451," *AFH,* XXXVIII (1945), p. 133, n. 2; *Constitutiones Segovienses, 1621,* p. 641.

[9] Marinus a Neukirchen says of the earlier Conventual *Constitutiones Sixtinae:* "Haec autem Statuta, quorum observantia quidem in comitiis an. 1485 Casali et an. 1488 Cremonae mandata fuit quaeque Minister generalis an. 1506 iussu Julii II una cum Constitutionibus Farineriis divulgavit, vix umquam in usum deducta sunt."—*De Capitulo Generali in Primo Ordine Seraphico,* p. 510.

[10] "Tenentur quoque Fratres ad omnia ieiunia, ad quae caeteri Christiani universaliter ab Ecclesia obligantur. At additur vigilia B. P. N. Francisci." —De Gubernatis, *Orbis Seraphicus,* III, 146.

[11] Herrera, *Legislación Eclesiástica sobre el Ayuno y la Abstinencia,* p. 58.

The Conventual *Constitutiones Urbanae* of 1628 commanded the Friars to fast on all vigils of the Blessed Virgin Mary, on the vigils of Saint Francis, Saint Bonaventure, and Saint Anthony, and on the vigils to which they are obliged in virtue of local custom or particular vows. By way of concession, these Constitutions relieved the Conventual Friars of the obligation of fasting when Christmas fell on a Friday.[12] The next subsequent edition of the *Constitutiones Urbanae,* the *Constitutiones Pio-Urbanae* of 1823, relaxed the obligation of fast and abstinence also when the Feast of Saint Francis fell on a Friday.[13]

With the promulgation of the Code of Canon Law, a new revision of the Conventual Constitutions became necessary. These latest Constitutions, published in 1932, are substantially an accommodation of the older *Constitutiones Pio-Urbanae* to the new law. In addition to what is set down by the common law and in the Franciscan Rule, these Constitutions oblige the Friars to fast, as heretofore, on the vigils of Saint Francis, Saint Bonaventure, and Saint Anthony; and on the vigils of the Immaculate Conception, the Nativity of the Blessed Virgin, the Presentation, the Annunciation, the Visitation, the Purification, and the Assumption. They impose a special obligation of abstinence for all Saturdays from the Feast of All Saints until Christmas.[14] This Saturday abstinence recalls the ancient practice of the Order,[15] and the still more

---

[12] *Constitutiones Urbanae Ordinis Fratrum Minorum S. Francisci Conventualium, 1628,* nn. 1, 2.

[13] *Constitutiones (Pio-) Urbanae Ordinis Minorum S. P. Francisci* (Romae, 1823), n. 1. Actually, the *Constitutiones Urbano-Clementinae* of 1771 were published before the *Constitutiones Pio-Urbanae,* but the *Constitutiones Urbano-Clementinae* had application only to the Observant Friars in France who had been aggregated to the Conventuals. Except in so far as they restricted the obligation of fasting to solely the vigils of the principal feasts of the Blessed Virgin, and failed to mention the obligation of fasting on certain vigils in virtue of local custom and particular vows, they were in agreement with the *Constitutiones Pio-Urbanae.—Constitutiones Urbanae (Urbano-Clementinae), 1771,* (Romae, 1894), p. 57, n. 1. Cf. also Marinus a Neukirchen, *De Capitulo Generali in Primo Ordine Seraphico,* p. 522.

[14] *Constitutiones Ordinis Fratrum Minorum Sancti Patris Francisci Conventualium, 1932,* nn. 317–319.

[15] *Chronica Fratris Jordani,* n. 11; "Constitutiones Narbonenses," *AFH,* XXXIV (1941), p. 56, n. 9.

ancient practice in the Church when all Saturdays were kept as days of fast.[16] The provision of the *Constitutiones Pio-Urbanae,* whereby the obligation to fast and to abstain ceased whenever Christmas or the Feast of Saint Francis fell on a Friday was renewed in these latest Conventual Constitutions.[17]

Section 3. The Constitutions of the Friars Minor of the Observant Families

With respect to the days on which the Friars are bound to fast, the several Constitutions of the various families of the Observant Franciscans are reluctant to depart from the ancient legislation of the *Constitutiones Narbonenses.* The *Constitutiones Segovienses* of 1621 were the first Observant Constitutions to impose further days of fast as of obligation. They commanded, in addition to what was called for by the older Constitutions, that the Friars were to fast on the vigils of Feasts of the Blessed Virgin Mary, and on the Vigil of the Ascension.[18] The *Constitutiones Segovienses* were of obligation for the ultramontane families of the Observant friars.[19] But even the Constitutions of the Reformed Franciscans of the Strict Observance refrained from imposing any new fasts or abstinences upon the Friars.[20]

The latest Constitutions published by the Franciscans of the Regular Observance as a group were the *Constitutiones Aloysianae* of 1889. In keeping with the conservative tradition of the Observant family, these Constitutions prescribed, apart from what

---

[16] Herrera, *Legislación Eclesiástica sobre el Ayuno y la Abstinencia,* pp. 20–28.

[17] *Constitutiones Ordinis Fratrum Minorum Sancti Patris Francisci Conventualium, 1932,* n. 318.

[18] See p. 641.

[19] Marinus a Neukirchen, *De Capitulo Generali in Primo Ordine Seraphico,* p. 516.

[20] Cf. "Constitutiones Calatayeronenses, 1595," De Gubernatis, *Orbis Seraphicus,* III, 565–566; *Statuti Generali delle Riforme de Minori Osservanti Cismontani, 1625* (Roma, 1626), pp. 48–49; *Statuta et Constitutiones Generales Familiae Cismontanae Ordinis S. Francisci Minorum Reformatorum, 1889* (Ad Claras Aquas, 1890), nn. 103–105; "Le Constitutioni Generali per le Provincie Riformate Cismontane, 1642," De Gubernatis, *Orbis Seraphicus,* IV, p. 97, nn. 23–25.

was demanded by the Rule and by general Church law, only that the Friars shall fast and abstain on the vigil of the Feast of Saint Francis.[21] This prescription of the *Constitutiones Aloysianae* is incorporated verbatim into the later *Constitutiones Generales Fratrum Minorum* of 1897,[22] 1913 [23] and 1922.[24] Although the latest *Constitutiones Generales Ordinis Fratrum Minorum* have dropped the simple wording of the *Constitutiones Aloysianae* in favor of a more thorough and a more precise treatment of the whole subject matter of fast and abstinence, the substance of their legislation is unchanged. In so far as actual days of fast and abstinence are concerned, aside from what is proposed in the Franciscan Rule and enacted in the Code of Canon Law, they prescribe only that the vigil of the Feast of Saint Francis should be kept as a day of fast and abstinence. The one new modification which they introduce into the older legislation of the Order is that they explicitly state that the Friars are not bound to fast when Christmas falls on a Friday.[25]

Section 4. The Constitutions of the Friars Minor Capuchin

The Constitutions of the Friars Minor Capuchin are also in accord with the conservative tradition of the Order with regard to the days of fast and abstinence which they prescribe. The first Capuchin Constitutions, the *Costituzioni di Albacina* of 1529, set aside Wednesday as a day of abstinence,[26] a disposition that has remained in the several redactions of the Constitutions to the present day.[27] The Constitutions of 1909 stated further that the

---

[21] "Praeter iéiunia ab Ecclesia et Regula praescripta, etiam Vigilia S. P. N. Francisci ab omnibus intra et extra Conventum ieiunio et abstinentia consecretur."—*Constitutiones Aloysianae, 1889* (Ad Claras Aquas, 1891), n. 174.

[22] See n. 174.

[23] See n. 197.

[24] See n. 198.

[25] Art. 181.

[26] "Costituzioni di Albacina, 1529," *Le Prime Costituzioni dei Frati Minori Cappuccini* (Roma, 1913), n. 40.

[27] "Le Constitutione deli Frati Minori Detti Capuccini, 1536," *Primigeniae Legislationis Ordinis Fratrum Minorum Capuccinorum Textus Originales* (Romae, 1928), n. 50; "Le Constitutioni de Frati Minori Detti Cappucini,

Friars should abstain on Wednesdays and Saturdays, or at least on one of these days.[28] This Wednesday and Saturday abstinence recalls the primitive observance in the Franciscan Order, when both Wednesday and Saturday were kept as days of fast.[29] It also brings to mind the ancient practice of the Christians, who kept Wednesday as a day of fast and who fasted on Saturdays in commemoration of our Lord's burial.[30]

The obligation to fast on the vigil of the Feast of Saint Francis is not mentioned in any of the Capuchin Constitutions until the edition of 1909. There it is prescribed that the vigil of the Feast of Saint Francis as well as the vigil of the Feast of the Immaculate Conception should be kept as days of fast and abstinence.[31] The most recent edition of the Constitutions of the Capuchin Order, those of 1925, renew the dispositions of the Constitutions of 1909. They repeat the prescription that the Friars should abstain on Wednesdays and Saturdays, or at least on one of these days; and, like the earlier Constitutions, they ordain that the Friars must observe fast and abstinence on the vigils of the Feast of Saint Francis and the Feast of the Immaculate Conception.[32]

Article II. Other Aspects of Fast and Abstinence

The preceding article was principally concerned with the days of fast and abstinence prescribed by the various Constitutions of the Order. The present article will treat all other aspects of fast and

---

1552," *Primigeniae Legislationis Ordinis Fratrum Minorum Capuccinorum Textus Originales,* n. 50; "Le Constitutioni de' Frati Minori Cappuccini, 1575," *Le Prime Costituzioni dei Frati Minori Cappuccini,* p. 55; *Constitutioni de Frati Minori Capucini, 1608* (Romae, 1609), p. 22; *Constitutioni dei Frati Minori Cappuccini, 1638* (Romae, 1638), p. 35; *Le Constituzioni dei Frati Minori Cappuccini, 1643* (Palermo, 1854), p. 42; *Constitutiones Fratrum Minorum S. Francisci Capuccinorum, 1909* (Romae, 1909), n. 67; *Constitutiones Fratrum Minorum Capuccinorum, 1925* (Romae, 1931), n. 69.

[28] *Constitutiones Fratrum Minorum S. Francisci Capuccinorum, 1909,* n. 67.

[29] *Chronica Fratris Jordani,* n. 11; "Constitutiones Narbonenses," *AFH,* XXXIV (1941), p. 56, n. 9.

[30] Wernz-Vidal, *Ius Canonicum,* IV, n. 520.

[31] *Constitutiones Fratrum Minorum S. Francisci Capuccinorum, 1909,* n. 67.

[32] *Constitutiones Fratrum Minorum Capuccinorum, 1925,* n. 69.

abstinence for which the aforesaid Constitutions present any legislation. As in the preceding article, the subject matter will be divided as follows: First the Constitutions previous to the division of the Order will be discussed, and then the Constitutions subsequent to that division. Among these latter, the Constitutions of the Order of Friars Minor Conventual will be treated first; then the Constitutions of the various groups in the Observant family; and, finally, the Constitutions of the Friars Minor Capuchin.

Section 1. The Early Constitutions

The Franciscan Rule states nothing about the manner in which the Friars should fast. It is completely silent on the whole question of abstinence. The many Constitutions that the Order has seen, however, amply make up for the deficiencies in the Rule. From the beginning they have contained detailed legislation on the many aspects of fast and abstinence.

The *Constitutiones Narbonenses,* the first general Constitutions of the Order, were clear and sweeping in their prescriptions concerning abstinence. They simply forbade that meat should ever be served in the houses of the Order. An exception was made only in favor of those Friars who were in delicate health, or who were actually suffering from some illness.[33] Similarly, lectors who were actually engaged in teaching were excepted.[34]

As a general rule, then, meat was not to be served in the dwellings of the Friars. During the Lents enjoined by the Rule, the Friars were bound further to restrict themselves to Lenten fare, which, according to the Constitutions, consisted of only fish and agricultural products.[35]

Any Friar who violated either the prescribed fast or the abstinence was to fast on bread and water as a punishment.[36] A special punishment was also to be meted out to Friars who partook of drink in cities or villages in which there were houses of the Order. Such Friars were to be obliged to take only water as their

[33] "Constitutiones Narbonenses, 1260," *AFH,* XXXIV (1941), p. 55, n. 4.

[34] "Constitutiones Narbonenses, 1260," *AFH,* XXXIV (1941), pp. 55–56, n. 4, footnote n. 8.

[35] "Constitutiones Narbonenses, 1260," *AFH,* XXXIV (1941), p. 55, n. 3.

[36] "Constitutiones Narbonenses, 1260," *AFH,* XXXIV (1941), p. 56, n. 6.

beverage at one meal for a whole week. The same punishment was to be applied to those who took meals other than with Church dignitaries, civil dignitaries, or religious men in places where there were houses of the Order.[37] As a precaution against the superfluous use of food, the *Constitutiones Narbonenses* directed that the Friars should be content with one course at every meal, and that they should make every effort to avoid the use of costly foods.[38] On Saturday, they were forbidden ever to use the blood or the fat of animals as a condiment.[39]

The *Constitutiones Parisienses* of 1291 directed that the Friars be content with a single refection in their friaries during the "Lent of Benediction." An exception was made only for the benefit of those who had a weak constitution, or who were in poor health, or who had undergone bloodletting.[40]

A relaxation of the former general prohibition of the Constitutions against the eating of meat in the houses of the Order[41] is found in the *Constitutiones Assisienses* of 1316, where it is stated simply that the Friars should be temperate and restricted in their use of meat, and that meat should not be served in the evening. The sick, however, were excepted, as were guests who had arrived on the day itself, provided that they had not eaten meat at noon. Friars who had preached during the afternoon, those who had been engaged in manual work, and those who had spent the entire day in questing for the benefit of the community were also exempt from the obligation.[42]

The Ordinances promulgated by Pope Benedict XII in 1336 applied to the Franciscan Order the ruling that was binding on the Cistercians. It forbade the Friars to eat meat at their chapters or in their own refectories.[43] In the *Constitutiones Assisienses* of 1354, however, there was a return to the milder injunction of the

[37] "Constitutiones Narbonenses, 1260," *AFH*, XXXIV (1941), p. 56, n. 8.

[38] "Constitutiones Narbonenses, 1260," *AFH*, XXXIV (1941), p. 56, n. 7.

[39] "Constitutiones Narbonenses, 1260," *AFH*, XXXIV (1941), p. 56, n. 9.

[40] "Constitutiones Parisienses, 1291," *AFH*, XXXIV (1941), p. 59, n. 1a.

[41] Cf. "Constitutiones Narbonenses, 1260," *AFH*, XXXIV (1941), p. 55, n. 4.

[42] "Constitutiones Assisienses, 1316," *AFH*, IV (1911), pp. 282–283, n. 4.

[43] "Ordinationes Sive Statuta Benedicti XII, 1336," *AFH*, XXX, (1937), pp. 338–340, n. 1, and footnote n. 6.

Constitutiones Assisienses of 1316.[44] The Friars were not forbidden to eat meat. Rather they were urged to be restrained and temperate in its use. They were forbidden to use meat in their refectories only in the evening.[45] All of these early Constitutions directed that on fast days the Friars should eat at the sixth hour, which, according to our way of reckoning, was at noon.[46] They likewise prescribed that the Friars should anticipate the Lenten fast by two days, beginning on Quinquagesima Sunday rather than on Ash Wednesday.[47]

Section 2. The Constitutions of the Friars Minor Conventual

The first legislation concerning the manner of fasting specifically for the Conventual Franciscans is found in the *Constitutiones Sixtinae* of 1469. These Constitutions forbade that the friary kitchen be opened in the evening during the time of Lent, and that any food should be cooked there for the brethren. They directed that transgressors should be punished.[48]

The *Constitutiones Alexandrinae* of 1500 were more detailed. They forbade the Friars to use milk products during the "Lent" preceding Christmas, after the manner in which the faithful in

---

[44] "Constitutiones Assisienses, 1316," *AFH*, IV (1911), pp. 282–283, n. 4.

[45] "Constitutiones Assisienses, 1354," *AFH*, XXXV (1942), p. 98, n. 4.

[46] "Constitutiones Narbonenses, 1260," *AFH*, XXXIV (1941), p. 55, n. 1; "Constitutiones Assisienses, 1279," *AFH*, XXXIV (1941), p. 59, n. 1; "Constitutiones Parisienses, 1292," *AFH*, XXXIV (1941), p. 59, n. 1; "Constitutiones Assisienses, 1316," *AFH*, IV (1911), p. 282, n. 1; "Statuta Caturcensia, 1337," *AFH*, XXX (1937), p. 132, n. 1; "Constitutiones Assisienses, 1340," *AFH*, VI (1913), p. 259, n. 1; "Statuta Lugdunensia, 1351," *AFH*, XXX (1937), p. 163, n. 1; "Constitutiones Assisienses, 1354," *AFH*, XXXV (1942), p. 97, n. 1.

[47] "Constitutiones Narbonenses, 1260," *AFH*, XXXIV (1941), p. 55, n. 3; "Constitutiones Assisienses, 1279," *AFH*, XXXIV (1941), p. 59, n. 3; "Constitutiones Parisienses, 1292," *AFH* XXXIV (1941), p. 59, n. 3; "Constitutiones Assisienses, 1316," *AFH* IV (1911), p. 282, n. 3; "Statuta Caturcensia, 1337," *AFH*, XXX (1937), p. 132, n. 3; "Constitutiones Assisienses, 1340," *AFH*, VI (1913), p. 259, n. 3; "Statuta Lugdunensia, 1351," *AFH*, XXX (1937), p. 163, n. 3; "Constitutiones Assisienses, 1354," *AFH*, XXXV (1942), p. 98, n. 3.

[48] "Constitutiones Sixtinae, 1469," *Miscellanea Franciscana*, XLV (1945), p. 124.

general were forbidden to use these foods during the Lent before Easter. In regions where olive oil could not be obtained, they permitted the Friars to use butter as a condiment during times of fast. They renewed the ordinance of the *Constitutiones Narbonenses*[49] which prohibited the use of blood and of animal fat as a condiment on Saturdays.

In the summer, so the *Constitutiones Alexandrinae* ordained, the main meal was to be served at noon; in the winter, at three o'clock in the afternoon. Guardians were reminded of their obligation to provide sufficient food at the principal meal during a season of fast, so that the Friars might be able to fast. The Friars who were subjects were exhorted on the other hand to be moderate and sparing in the use of food.[50] The norm set down in the *Constitutiones Pio-Urbanae* in 1823 stated that a portion of at least six ounces of meat was to be served to every Friar at dinner and at supper outside of the times of fast. Fish, fruits, and vegetables were to be served in suitable quantity.[51] In places where there was a friary of the Order, the Friars were not permitted to eat elsewhere, except for a reasonable cause, and then only with ecclesiastical prelates, civil dignitaries, or religious men,[52] a provision which was found already in the *Constitutiones Narbonenses.*[53] The *Constitutiones Alexandrinae* were the first to invoke a principle which later became characteristic of all the Constitutions of the Conventual Franciscans, namely that all professed Friars, regardless of age, are bound to the fasts of the Rule.[54]

A public fast on bread and water was prescribed in the *Consti-*

---

[49] "Constitutiones Narbonenses, 1260," *AFH,* XXXIV (1941), p. 56, n. 9.

[50] "Constitutiones Alexandrinae, 1500," De Gubernatis, *Orbis Seraphicus,* III, 146–147; *Constitutiones Urbanae, 1628,* pp. 103–104, n. 3, n. 6; *Constitutiones Urbanae (Urbano-Clementinae), 1771,* pp. 57–58, n. 2, n. 3; *Constitutiones (Pio-) Urbanae, 1823,* pp. 105–106, n. 3, n. 6.

[51] *Constitutiones (Pio-) Urbanae, 1823,* p. 105, n. 3.

[52] "Constitutiones Alexandrinae, 1500," De Gubernatis, *Orbis Seraphicus,* III, 147.

[53] "Constitutiones Narbonenses, 1260," *AFH,* XXXIV (1941), p. 56, n. 8.

[54] "Constitutiones Alexandrinae, 1500," De Gubernatis, *Orbis Seraphicus,* III, 146; *Constitutiones Urbanae, 1628,* pp. 103–104, n. 4; *Constitutiones (Pio-) Urbanae, 1823,* p. 105, n. 4; *Constitutiones Ordinis Fratrum Minorum Sancti Patris Francisci Conventualium, 1932,* n. 323.

tutiones Urbanae of 1628 and in the *Constitutiones Pio-Urbanae* of 1823 for those who violated the fast.[55] The earlier *Constitutiones Pianae* had prescribed that such violators be incarcerated as well.[56] The above mentioned Constitutions of 1628 and 1823 also demanded that a grave punishment be inflicted upon those who ate forbidden foods during a season of fast, and upon Superiors who, without the authorization of the Minister General, the Minister Provincial, or a Guardian, had given permission to do so.[57]

In the Conventual Constitutions of 1932, very little is set down concerning fast and abstinence which is not already contained in the common law or in the Rule. The determination of the quality and the quantity of the food permissible during a time of fast is left to local custom.[58] The obligation of all professed Friars, regardless of age or condition, to observe the fasts imposed by the Rule and the Constitutions is restated,[59] and it is ordered that the Friars should be permitted to eat in the homes of seculars only on rare occasions.[60]

Section 3. The Constitutions of the Friars Minor of the Observant Families

As a general rule, the various Constitutions which were in force among the several families of the Observant Franciscans at different times have directed the Friars to keep the fasts imposed by the Rule and by the Church in the same manner as Christians in general keep the fasts to which they are obliged.[61] Therefore, in

[55] *Constitutiones Urbanae, 1628,* p. 104, n. 3; *Constitutiones Pio-Urbanae, 1823,* p. 104, n. 3. Cf. also the "Constitutiones Narbonenses, 1260," *AFH,* XXXIV (1941), pp. 55–56.

[56] "Constitutiones Pianae, 1565," *Magnum Bullarium Romanum* (18 vols., Luxemburgi, 1727–1754), II, 177.

[57] *Constitutiones Urbanae, 1628,* pp. 103–104, n. 4; *Constitutiones (Pio-) Urbanae, 1823,* p. 105, n. 4.

[58] *Constitutiones Ordinis Fratrum Minorum Sancti Patris Francisci Conventualium, 1932,* n. 320.

[59] *Constitutiones Ordinis Fratrum Minorum Sancti Patris Francisci Conventualium, 1932,* n. 323.

[60] *Constitutiones Ordinis Fratrum Minorum Sancti Patris Francisci Conventualium, 1932,* n. 338.

[61] "Constitutiones Capistranenses, 1443," De Gubernatis, *Orbis Seraphicus,*

keeping with what was formerly the general practice of the Church,[62] the older Constitutions commonly forbade the Friars to eat meat, milk products, eggs, and cheese during seasons of fast.[63] The *Statuta Generalia* of 1553 of the Cismontane Friars of the Regular Observance legislated that those who ate such forbidden foods were to be compelled to wear the hood of the novices.[64] Later Constitutions deprived such transgressors of their right of suffrage,[65] or forbade their promotion to any office in the Order.[66] They also stated that Guardians who illicitly provided their subjects with such forbidden foods were to be deposed from office.[67] Only in a case of genuine necessity, to which a physician had previously attested, could a Friar, with the approval of his Superior, licitly eat prohibited foods during a time of fast. When such permission was granted, the Friars could not make use of it in the public refectory, but only in the infirmary.[68]

III, 97; *Constitutiones Aloysianae, 1889,* n. 173; *Statuta et Constitutiones Generales Familiae Cismontanae Ordinis S. Francisci Minorum Reformatorum, 1889,* n. 103; *Constitutiones Generales Fratrum Minorum, 1897,* n. 173; *Constitutiones Generales Ordinis Fratrum Minorum, 1953,* art. 182.

[62] Herrera, *Legislación Eclesiástica sobre el Ayuno y la Abstinencia,* pp. 93–95.

[63] *Constitutiones Salmanticenses, 1553* (Romae, 1576), p. 15; "Constitutiones Vallisoletanae, 1593," De Gubernatis, *Orbis Seraphicus,* III, 440; *Constitutiones Romanae, 1642* (Romae, 1642), p. 46, n. 1; *Constitutiones Sambucanae, 1663* (Romae, 1663), p. 72, n. 1; *Constitutiones Capistranae, 1768* (Romae, 1827), n. 222; *Constitutiones Aloysianae, 1889,* n. 173; *Statuti Generali delle Riforme de Minori Osservanti Cismontani, 1625,* p. 48; "Le Constitutioni Generali per le Provincie Riformate Cismontane, 1642," De Gubernatis, *Orbis Seraphicus,* IV, p. 97, n. 23.

[64] *Statuta Generalia seu Constitutiones Salmanticenses, 1553,* p. 15.

[65] "Constitutiones Vallisoletanae, 1593," De Gubernatis, *Orbis Seraphicus,* III, 440–441; *Constitutiones Romanae, 1642,* p. 46, n. 1; *Constitutiones Sambucanae, 1663,* p. 72, n. 1; *Constitutiones Capistranae, 1768,* n. 222.

[66] *Constitutiones Capistranae, 1768,* n. 222.

[67] *Constitutiones Salmanticenses, 1553,* p. 15; "Constitutiones Vallisoletanae, 1593," De Gubernatis, *Orbis Seraphicus,* III, 440; *Constitutiones Romanae, 1642,* p. 46, n. 1; *Constitutiones Sambucanae, 1663,* p. 72, n. 1; *Constitutiones Capistranae, 1768,* n. 222.

[68] "Constitutiones Vallisoletanae, 1593," De Gubernatis, *Orbis Seraphicus,* III, 440; *Constitutiones Romanae, 1642,* p. 46; *Constitutiones Sambucanae, 1663,* n. 1; *Constitutiones Capistranae, 1768,* n. 222.

Outside the times of fast, when meat was permitted, the friars were exhorted to be moderate in its use, lest they give scandal. Meat was to be served only once a day. The sick, travelers, preachers, and those who had spent the day laboring for the common good, however, were permitted to have it more often.[69] The *Constitutiones Calatayeronenses* of 1595 allowed the Reformed Franciscans of the Italian provinces to eat meat only when it was spontaneously offered to them. They strictly forbade the Friars to quest for it or to obtain it by purchase.[70]

Frequently the Constitutions called attention to the obligation of leading the perfect common life with regard to food.[71] For that reason they forbade Guardians to allow their subjects to take meals away from the community, except for a reasonable cause.[72] They decreed that any Friar who broke the fast, except in case of a necessity which had been previously approved by his Superior, should be severely punished.[73] For their part, on the other hand, Superiors were commanded to provide a sufficiency of licit foods, so that the Friars would be able to maintain the fast in all its rigor.[74]

On days of fast the Observant Friars were forbidden to prepare

[69] "Constitutiones Capistranae, 1443," De Gubernatis, *Orbis Seraphicus,* III, 97–98; "Constitutiones Barcinonenses, 1451," *AFH,* XXXVIII (1945), p. 133, n. 4; *Constitutiones Segovienses, 1621,* p. 641.

[70] "Constitutiones Calatayeronenses, 1595," De Gubernatis, *Orbis Seraphicus,* III, 565.

[71] *Constitutiones Salmanticenses, 1553,* p. 15; "Constitutiones Vallisoletanae, 1593," De Gubernatis, *Orbis Seraphicus,* III, 440; *Constitutiones Romanae, 1642,* pp. 46–47, n. 3, n. 4; *Constitutiones Sambucanae, 1663,* pp. 72–73, n. 3, n. 4.

[72] *Constitutiones Salmanticenses, 1553,* p. 15; "Constitutiones Vallisoletanae, 1593," De Gubernatis, *Orbis Seraphicus,* III, 440; *Constitutiones Segovienses, 1621,* p. 641; "Constitutiones Calatayeronenses, 1595," De Gubernatis, *Orbis Seraphicus,* III, 565.

[73] "Constitutiones Vallisoletanae, 1593," De Gubernatis, *Orbis Seraphicus,* III, 440; *Constitutiones Romanae, 1642,* p. 47, n. 6; *Constitutiones Sambucanae, 1663,* p. 73, n. 6; *Constitutiones Aloysianae, 1889,* n. 178.

[74] *Constitutiones Salmanticenses, 1553,* p. 15; "Constitutiones Vallisoletanae, 1593," De Gubernatis, *Orbis Seraphicus,* III, 440; *Constitutiones Romanae, 1642,* p. 46, n. 2; *Constitutiones Sambucanae, 1663,* p. 72, n. 2; *Constitutiones Aloysianae, 1889,* n. 177.

any cooked food for the collation, except for guests who had arrived on that same day, and who both needed and requested such food.[75] Some of the Constitutions laid special emphasis on the Friday fast, stating that the Friars who took supper on that day, even in their own cells or in the guest house, were to be punished as manifest transgressors of the Rule.[76]

The *Constitutiones Segovienses,* which pertained to the ultramontane branch of the Observant Franciscans, ruled that, for the purpose of preventing disorders, and in order to obtain the paternal blessing during the "Lent of Benediction," all the Friars were to be satisfied with a single refection. These same Constitutions stated that a Superior who was unable to eat the same food as the rest of the community was to be relieved of his office and was to be considered incapable of holding such an office in the future.[77]

The *Constitutiones Calatayeronenses* of the Reformed Franciscans in Italy exhorted the Friars to fast on bread and water while kneeling in the refectory on all the Fridays in March.[78] Later Constitutions of this same branch of the Order commanded Guardians, in keeping with holy poverty, to provide for the needs of those who wished to keep the "'Lents" of the Holy Spirit, of the Assumption, or of Saint Michael.[79]

The *Constitutiones Aloysianae* of 1889, which united the cismontane and the ultramontane branches of the Franciscans of the Regular Observance under a common legislation, reflected a change which had gradually taken place in the manner of observing the general law of fast when they permitted the Friars to use milk

[75] *Constitutiones Romanae, 1642,* p. 46, n. 2; *Constitutiones Sambucanae, 1663,* p. 72, n. 2; *Constitutiones Aloysianae, 1889,* n. 177.

[76] *Constitutiones Sambucanae, 1663,* p. 73, n. 7; *Constitutiones Capistranae, 1768,* n. 223.

[77] *Constitutiones Segovienses, 1621,* p. 641.

[78] "Constitutiones Calatayeronenses, 1595," De Gubernatis, *Orbis Seraphicus,* III, 566.

[79] *Statuti Generali delle Riforme de Minori Osservanti Cismontani, 1625,* p. 49; "Le Constitutioni Generali per le Provincie Riformate Cismontane, 1642," De Gubernatis, *Orbis Seraphicus,* IV, 97; *Constitutiones Generales Familiae Cismontanae Ordinis S. Francisci Minorum Reformatorum, 1889,* n. 105.

products during a time of fast whenever local custom allowed it.[80] The Constitutions of the cismontane branch of the Reformed Franciscans of that same year also included this modification of the traditional practice.[81] The *Constitutiones Aloysianae* urged Guardians to vigilance lest their subjects violate the law of the fast, and at the same time commanded them to make every provision for its observance.[82]

The first Constitutions of the Order of Friars Minor published after the Leonine Union, the *Constitutiones Generales Fratrum Minorum* of 1897, contained almost the same legislation as the *Constitutiones Aloysianae*. They also permitted the eating of milk products during a time of fast whenever legitimate custom allowed it.[83]

The legislation on fast and abstinence of the *Constitutiones Generales Fratrum Minorum* of 1913 [84] and 1922,[85] was in close harmony with the legislation of the previous Constitutions, except that they omitted all reference to the quality of food to which the Friars were to attend during a season of fast.

An extensive and precise treatment of fast and abstinence is found in the most recent edition of the Constitutions of the Order of Friars Minor, but the special legislation concerning the manner of fasting is very brief. The Constitutions merely state that, with regard to the quantity and the quality of food they are permitted to take on a day of fast, the Friars may follow local custom,[86] and that, in accordance with Canon Law, the Friars may eat meat only once on a fast day.[87]

Section 4. The Constitutions of the Friars Minor Capuchin

The dispositions of their early Constitutions concerning fast and abstinence are a mirror of the type of life lived by the first

---

80 *Constitutiones Aloysianae, 1889,* n. 173.

81 *Constitutiones Generales Familiae Cismontanae Ordinis S. Francisci Minorum Reformatorum, 1889,* n. 103.

82 *Constitutiones Aloysianae, 1889,* n. 177.

83 *Constitutiones Generales Fratrum Minorum, 1897,* n. 173.

84 *Constitutiones Generales Fratrum Minorum, 1913,* n. 197, n. 198, n. 199.

85 *Constitutiones Generales Fratrum Minorum, 1922,* nn. 198, 199, 200.

86 *Constitutiones Generales Ordinis Fratrum Minorum, 1953,* art. 182, § 1.

87 *Constitutiones Generales Ordinis Fratrum Minorum, 1953,* art. 182, § 2.

Capuchin Friars. These Constitutions permitted only one course of food or a soup to be served at each meal. During a season of fast, however, the Constitutions were somewhat more indulgent. They allowed the Friars to take a second dish consisting of a salad, which could be either cooked or raw. If it should happen that a little fish or some other food had been donated, the Constitutions forbade the Friars to use it at table if they would thereby violate the regulation restricting them to two courses.[88] Whenever wine was served at table, the Constitutions decreed that it should be well watered.[89]

All the Friars were commanded to partake of a common table. An exception was granted only in favor of the sick, the travelers, and those who were in delicate health.[90] If any Friar wished to

---

[88] "Costituzioni di Albacina, 1529," *Le Prime Costituzioni dei Frati Minori Cappuccini,* n. 12; "Le Constitutione deli Frati Minori Detti Capuccini, 1536," *Primigeniae Legislationis Ordinis Fratrum Minorum Capuccinorum Textus Originales,* n. 51; "Le Constitutioni de Frati Minori Detti Cappucini, 1552," *Primigeniae Legislationis Ordinis Fratrum Minorum Capuccinorum Textus Originales,* n. 51; "Le Constitutioni de' Frati Minori Cappuccini, 1575," *Le Prime Costituzioni dei Frati Minori Cappuccini,* p. 55; *Constitutioni de Frati Minori Capucini, 1608,* p. 22; *Constitutioni dei Frati Minori Cappuccini, 1638,* p. 36; *Le Constituzioni dei Frati Minori Cappuccini, 1643,* p. 42.

[89] "Costituzioni di Albacina, 1529," *Le Prime Costituzioni dei Frati Minori Cappuccini,* n. 13; "Le Constitutione deli Frati Minori Detti Capuccini, 1536," *Primigeniae Legislationis Ordinis Fratrum Minorum Capuccinorum Textus Originales,* n. 52; "Le Constitutioni de Frati Minori Detti Cappucini, 1552," *Primigeniae Legislationis Ordinis Fratrum Minorum Capuccinorum Textus Originales,* n. 52; "Le Constituzioni dei Frati Minori Cappuccini, 1575," *Le Prime Costituzioni dei Frati Minori Cappuccini,* p. 56; *Constitutioni de Frati Minori Capucini, 1608,* p. 22; *Constitutioni dei Frati Minori Cappuccini, 1638,* p. 36; *Le Constituzioni dei Frati Minori Cappuccini, 1643,* p. 42; *Constitutiones Fratrum Minorum S. Francisci Capuccinorum, 1909,* n. 69; *Constitutiones Fratrum Minorum Capuccinorum, 1925,* n. 71.

[90] "Le Constitutione deli Frati Minori Detti Capuccini, 1536," *Primigeniae Legislationis Ordinis Fratrum Minorum Capuccinorum Textus Originales,* n. 53; "Le Constitutioni de Frati Minori Detti Cappucini, 1552," *Primigeniae Legislationis Ordinis Fratrum Minorum Capuccinorum Textus Originales,* n. 53; "Le Constitutioni de' Frati Minori Capuccini, 1575," *Le Prime Costituzioni dei Frati Minori Cappuccini,* p. 56; *Constitutioni de Frati Minori Capucini, 1608,* p. 22; *Constitutioni dei Frati Minori Cappuccini, 1638,* p. 37;

abstain from wine, from meat, or from some other food, or if he wished to fast more often than was customary, the Constitutions admonished Superiors prudently to encourage such practices, if they saw that they would not be harmful to the Friar's health, and provided that he ate with the community.[91]

The Constitutions of 1536 and those of 1552 forbade the Friars to beg for costly foods or to receive such foods, unless they were necessary for the sick. If costly foods were offered to them, they were humbly to refuse them, or, with the consent of the donor, they were to give them to the poor.[92] The Constitutions of 1608 manifested the gradual adjustment that had taken place from the primitive hermitical life of the first Capuchins to a more active apostolic life, when for the first time in Capuchin legislation they incorporated a prohibition that barred the Friars from taking meals outside the houses of the Order without the permission of their Superior.[93] Such a question could hardly have arisen in a community of hermits, but it could hardly remain absent from a community that was engaged in active work among the faithful.

Le Constituzioni dei Frati Minori Cappuccini, 1643, p. 43; *Constitutiones Fratrum Minorum S. Francisci Capuccinorum, 1909,* n. 69; *Constitutiones Fratrum Minorum Capuccinorum, 1925,* n. 71.

[91] "Costituzioni di Albacina, 1529," *Le Prime Costituzioni dei Frati Minori Cappuccini,* n. 13, n. 14; "Le Constitutione deli Frati Minori Detti Capuccini, 1536," *Primigeniae Legislationis Ordinis Fratrum Minorum Capuccinorum Textus Originales,* n. 53; "Le Constitutioni de Frati Minori Detti Cappucini, 1552," *Primigeniae Legislationis Ordinis Fratrum Minorum Capuccinorum Textus Originales,* n. 53; "Le Constitutioni de' Frati Minori Cappucini, 1575," *Le Prime Costituzioni dei Frati Minori Cappuccini,* p. 56; *Constitutioni de Frati Minori Capuccini, 1608,* p. 22; *Constitutioni dei Frati Minori Cappuccini, 1638,* p. 37; *Le Constituzioni dei Frati Minori Cappuccini, 1643,* p. 43; *Constitutiones Fratrum Minorum S. Francisci Capuccinorum, 1909,* n. 69; *Constitutiones Fratrum Minorum Capuccinorum, 1925,* n. 71.

[92] "Le Constitutione deli Frati Minori Detti Capuccini, 1536," *Primigeniae Legislationis Ordinis Fratrum Minorum Capuccinorum Textus Originales,* n. 54; "Le Constitutioni de Frati Minori Detti Cappucini, 1552," *Primigeniae Legislationis Ordinis Fratrum Minorum Capuccinorum Textus Originales,* n. 54.

[93] *Constitutioni de Frati Minori Capucini, 1608,* p. 23. See also: *Le Constituzioni dei Frati Minori Cappuccini, 1643,* p. 43; *Constitutiones Fratrum Minorum S. Francisci Capuccinorum, 1909,* n. 71; *Constitutiones Fratrum Minorum Capuccinorum, 1925,* n. 74.

The Constitutions of 1638 were the first that explicitly excluded the use of eggs, cheese, butter, and other milk products during the fasts to which the Friars were bound, whether from the Rule or from the Church's common law, although they permitted the use of butter as a condiment in places where oil was unobtainable, provided that such use had been sanctioned either through an indult from the Holy See or through custom. In actual practice, however, this explicit prohibition changed nothing, for even in the absence of any previous positive legislation in their Constitutions the Capuchins had always been forbidden the use of such foods during a season of fast in virtue of general Church law [94] and in virtue of the customary usage of the Order. That such a usage really existed can be gathered from the fact that, in the year 1583, Pope Gregory XIII granted to the Friars of the Capuchin Province of Switzerland the permission to eat milk products during a time of fast according to the customs of the region.[95] For the collation on a fast day, these same Constitutions of 1638 allowed only fruit, or, if fruit could not be had, bread. In no case did they permit fruit and bread to be served at the same collation. Superiors were ordered to punish those who transgressed the Constitutions in the matter of fast and abstinence. This punishment was to be the discipline; and it was to be administered in the public refectory.[96]

The former prohibition to eat milk products during a season of fast underwent a notable modification in the Constitutions of 1909, which made a definite distinction between what was permitted during a regular fast and what was permitted during an ecclesiastical fast. During fasts imposed in the Rule, these Constitutions obliged the Friars to abstain from meat and milk products, unless they had received a legitimate dispensation from the Holy See, or unless they dwelt in regions where approved customs, or dispensations which pertained also to the Friars Minor, conceded the use of milk products. They were always forbidden, however,

---

[94] Herrera, *Legislación Eclesiástica sobre el Ayuno y la Abstinencia,* pp. 93–95.

[95] *Bullarium Capuccinorum* (Vols. I–VII, Romae, 1740–1752; Vols. VIII–X, Oeniponte, 1883–1884), IV, 31.

[96] *Constitutioni dei Frati Minori Cappuccini, 1638,* n. 36, n. 37.

to eat meat during the times of the fasts imposed in the Rule. On the other hand, during the times of fasts imposed by the Church's common law, the Friars were permitted to take advantage of the indults and the decrees of the Holy See which had been given for the region in which they resided.[97]

According to the decree of approval issued by the Sacred Congregation of Religious, the latest redaction of the Capuchin Constitutions, that of 1925, is an accommodation of the Constitutions of 1909 to the legislation of the Code of Canon Law.[98] The changes found in these new Constitutions, therefore, result principally from the changes in the common law. In keeping with the dispositions of the new law, the Constitutions of 1925 drop the ancient legislation which prohibited the use of eggs and milk products during a time of fast. With regard to the quality and the quantity of food allowed, even during times of fast imposed in the Rule, they permit the Friars to follow the common law of the Code, and to benefit through the papal indults granted for certain regions, or from the approved customs of the place. In keeping with Franciscan poverty, they state that, within the friary, only what is sufficient is to be served at table.[99] Finally, they decree that those who habitually violate the fasts and abstinences enacted by the Church or imposed in the Rule should be punished by being deprived of active and passive electoral rights for two years. If the nature of the violative practice calls for it, the Constitutions insist on an even more severe punishment.[100]

---

[97] *Constitutiones Fratrum Minorum S. Francisci Capuccinorum, 1909,* n. 68.

[98] See the *Decretum* through which they were approved. Cf. *Constitutiones Fratrum Minorum Capuccinorum, 1925* (editio altera, Romae, Typis Polyglottis Vaticanis, 1931), p. 23.

[99] *Constitutiones Fratrum Minorum Capuccinorum, 1925,* n. 70.

[100] *Constitutiones Fratrum Minorum Capuccinorum, 1925,* n. 69.

CHAPTER III

OTHER LEGISLATION

INTRODUCTION

As the title to this chapter indicates, it will treat primarily of legislation touching upon the discipline of fast and abstinence within the Franciscan Order other than that which is contained in the Rule and the Constitutions. The first article of the chapter will deal with some of the more important pre-Code indults which have a bearing on that discipline. The second article will discuss the relationship of the law of the Code to the special law of the Order with regard to fast and abstinence, first in a general way, and then with reference to the dispensatory powers of local ordinaries. Continuing the discussion of dispensations, the third article will treat of the special faculties for dispensing which local ordinaries have enjoyed since 1941 with respect to religious. The fourth and last article will conclude this discussion of dispensations by explaining the dispensatory powers of Superiors within the Order.

ARTICLE I. INDULTS PREVIOUS TO THE CODE

Section 1. Earlier Indults

Before the Code of Canon Law established a uniform practice for the entire Church, the law concerning the quality of foods permissible during a time of fast admitted of many variations. The ancient law of the Church had excluded the use not only of meat, but of all other foods that were animal in origin. Thus eggs and all types of milk products were forbidden, since they traced their origin to animals.[1]

The Church applied this severe discipline primarily to the Lent before Easter, for Christians had always regarded this Lent as the

[1] Wernz-Vidal, *Ius Canonicum,* IV, n. 524.

principal fast of the Church.[2] By way of analogy, the Franciscans applied it also to the principal fast imposed in their Rule, the "Lent" before Christmas. So deeply and firmly entrenched did this observance become in the Order that, even after the faithful had begun to observe the Lent before Easter in a less rigorous way, the Friars continued to be obliged to the ancient usage during the "Lent" of the Rule.[3] It was not until the legislation of the Order had been revised and brought into conformity with both the letter and the spirit of the law of the Code that the Friars were generally permitted to follow a more lenient practice. Today, members of all three branches of the Order are permitted to conform to local usage with regard to both the quantity and the quality of foods permissible even during fasts imposed in the Rule.[4]

The transition from the former rigorous law concerning the quality of foods to the more benign law of the present day was brought about gradually. It was introduced, not by any general legislative act, but by a series of local and particular concessions on the part of the Holy See. Unfortunately for the general discipline of the Church, these concessions were frequently granted without much concern for uniformity or for system. One of the chief benefits of the Code was to bring about a certain uniformity and to establish a reasonably common discipline for the entire Church.

It would be difficult, if not impossible, to trace a precise and ordered development of the law of fast and abstinence in the Franciscan Order. The principal difficulty lies in this that, like the development in the Church at large, it followed a local pattern. As a normal policy, the Apostolic See granted indults to particular provinces, rather than to the Order as a whole. Nevertheless, a survey of some of these indults does show a general tendency toward a more lenient discipline.

---

[2] Herrera, *Legislación Eclesiástica sobre el Ayuno y la Abstinencia*, p. 93.

[3] Cf. *Constitutiones Fratrum Minorum S. Francisci Capuccinorum, 1909*, n. 68.

[4] *Regula et Constitutiones Generales Ordinis Fratrum Minorum, 1953*, art. 182, § 1; art. 184, § 1; *Constitutiones Ordinis Fratrum Minorum Sancti Patris Francisci Conventualium, 1932*, n. 320; *Constitutiones Fratrum Minorum Capuccinorum, 1925*, n. 70.

Already in the early days of the Capuchin reform, in the year 1583, Pope Gregory XIII granted to the Friars in Switzerland the faculty to eat milk products during seasons of fast according to the customs of the country.[5] The same concession was extended to the Friars in Poland in the year 1781.[6] It is interesting to read that it was only as late as the year 1641 that Pope Urban VIII (1623–1644) granted to the Capuchin Friars of the Province of Palermo permission to eat meat in the friaries of the Province.[7] Previous to that time it had been entirely forbidden.

In the year 1786 the German Provincial Superiors received the faculty to dispense from the prohibition of the eating of meat during Lent for the benefit of their subjects who were dwelling, under the merit of obedience, outside a house of the Order.[8] This concession was something quite out of the ordinary. It is the first recorded extensive relaxation in the Capuchin Order of the law prohibiting the eating of meat during Lent. Doubtless, the monumental pronouncements on fasting by Pope Benedict XIV (1740–1758) of a few years before[9] facilitated the granting of this faculty. In the legislation that he enacted, Pope Benedict definitely established the principle that the primary and principal element of fasting is the prohibition to eat more than one full meal a day. Subsequent to his reign, the Holy See granted dispensations from the law regarding the quality of foods with increasing frequency and greater generosity.[10] In 1873 the Minister General of the Capuchins received the very broad faculty of permitting his subjects the use of meat during Advent in any case of true necessity.[11]

---

[5] *Bullarium Capuccinorum,* IV, 31.

[6] *Bullarium Capuccinorum,* IX, 151.

[7] *Bullarium Capuccinorum,* III, 155.

[8] *Bullarium Capuccinorum,* IX, 151.

[9] Benedictus XIV, ep. encycl. *Non ambigimus,* 30 maii 1741—*Codicis Iuris Canonici Fontes,* cura Emi Petri Card. Gasparri editi (9 vols., Romae [later Civitate Vaticana]: Typis Polyglottis Vaticanis, 1923–1939) (Vols. VII–IX ed. cura et studio Emi Iustiniani Card. Serédi), n. 308 (hereafter cited *Fontes*).

[10] Cf. *Bullarium Capuccinorum,* IX, 207; 254; X, 46; 90; 307.

[11] *Bullarium Capuccinorum,* X, 661.

Section 2. Later Indults

In the decades immediately preceding the publication of the Code, a number of rescripts and decrees dealing with the fasts and abstinences of religious were given by the Holy See, some of which were of notable consequence for the Franciscan Order. If those whose purpose was merely temporary or local are set aside, four rescripts can be singled out as of the greatest importance. Only one of these rescripts, however, was issued to the Superiors of all three branches of the Franciscan Order. One was issued to the Minister General of the Observant Franciscans alone, another to one of the Observant Ministers Provincial, and the fourth to the Superior General of the Congregation of the Mission. Two of the rescripts, therefore, were special in character, inasmuch as they were issued only to Superiors of the Observant Franciscan family. One was special in that it was issued to the Superior of an entirely different religious Institute. Nevertheless, according to the teaching of pre-Code canonists, all four were of universal application within the Franciscan Order. Even though they were formally special, they were materially general in that they laid down principles that were applicable to all three Franciscan families. Therefore, they were of obligation for all.[12] The primary function of all four of these rescripts, since they contained authentic interpretations of the law, was to determine the effect that dispensations when granted by authorities outside the Order could have on the Friars' obligation to fast or to abstain.

The first of these rescripts was granted on December 20, 1871, at the request of Father Bernardine of Port Romantino, then the Minister General of the Observant Franciscans, by the Sacred Congregation of the Holy Office. It follows:

> Having first kissed your most holy feet, Most Blessed Father, Fr. Bernardine of Port Romantino, Minister General of the Order of Minors, in order to dispel the mental anxieties of his Friars dwelling in all parts of the world, and, at the same time, in order to allay their infirmity, most humbly begs Your Holiness to deign to declare or to concede that the indults dealing with the fast

[12] Cf. Wernz, *Ius Decretalium* (6 vols. in 10, Vol. 1, 2. ed., Romae: Prati, 1905), n. 146, IV.

of Lent and with the other fasts enjoined on all the faithful during the year which are promulgated by bishops in their respective dioceses comprehend also regulars, notwithstanding the fact that the bishops make no mention of regulars in the aforesaid indults (as is usually the case in almost all dioceses outside of Italy), and although in some dioceses there is a condition imposed upon the users of the indult which cannot in any way be met by regulars, namely, the giving and the depositing in the Episcopal Curia of a certain sum of money to be used for pious purposes. For which favor.

On Wednesday, December 20, 1871, the Sacred Congregation of the Holy Office saw fit to reply: "Regulars who are not bound by a special vow to abstain from meat benefit by the indult regarding the quality of foods when promulgated for the faithful by local ordinaries in the name of the Apostolic See both in the time of Lent and during the course of the year." [13]

There are four points worth noting in this indult:

1) The Franciscans could make use of dispensations from fasts which were imposed by general Church law, but not from those which were imposed by the law of the Order.

The petition asked for a clarification only with regard to the

---

[13] "Bm̃e Pater, Fr. Bernardinus a Portu Romantino Minister Generalis Ordinis Minorum, praemisso osculo SS. Pedum, humillime supplicat S. V. quatenus, ad tollendas suorum Fratrum ubique terrarum existentium animi anxietates, simulque ad subveniendum eorum infirmitati, declarare, aut concedere dignetur, indulta quae ab Episcopis, in respectivis Dioecesibus, *quoad ieiunium S. Quadragesimae et alia ieiunia infra annum omnibus fidelibus* iniuncta promulgantur, comprehendere etiam Regulares, non obstante quod Episcopi in praefatis indultis de Regularibus nullam mentionem faciant (prout usuvenit in fere omnibus dioecesibus extra Italiam), et quamvis in aliquibus dioecesibus ea conditio Indulto utentibus imponatur, quae a Regularibus impleri nullatenus potest, erogandi scilicet, et apud Curiam Episcopalem deponendi aliquam pecuniae summam, in pia opera impendendam. Pro qua gratia.

Fer. IV die 20 Decembris 1871 Sacra Congregatio S. Officii respondere censuit, Regulares speciali voto abstinentiae a carnibus non adstrictos, gaudere Indulto circa observantiam ciborum *tempore Quadragesimae et per annum pro fidelibus promulgato* ab Ordinariis locorum nomine Sanctae Sedis Apostolicae."—Mocchegiani, *Iurisprudentia Ecclesiastica,* II, 35–36; Albertus a Bulsano, *Expositio Regulae FF. Minorum,* 1932, p. 251–252.

fast of Lent and other fasts which are enjoined upon all the faithful during the year. The Holy See must be presumed to have given its answer within the limits of the submitted petition, so that it did not grant anything beyond the request. Accordingly the fasts imposed in the Franciscan Rule and in the Constitutions were not included within the terms of the indult.

2) The indult was concerned only with the *quality* of the foods that are permitted during a time of fast.

In virtue of this indult, therefore, the Friars could not take advantage of a complete dispensation from the obligation of fast.

3) The indults had to be granted by local ordinaries *in the name of the Apostolic See.*

4) The Franciscans could take advantage of them even when the indults made no mention of Regulars.

With certain modifications, the substance of this indult of 1871 is found in the Observant Constitutions of 1889,[14] of 1897,[15] and of 1953;[16] in the Capuchin Constitutions of 1909[17] and 1925;[18] and in the Conventual Constitutions of 1932.[19]

On January 4, 1892, the Supreme Roman and Universal Inquisition gave answer to the following doubt proposed by the Minister Provincial of the Franciscan Province of Bologna:

> Most Blessed Father,
>
> Mindful of the influenza that rages also in Parma, the Lord Bishop published an indult couched in the following terms: "As long as the influenza endures, that is the contagious infection which is becoming ever more widespread, We, by the authority of Rome, declare that the obligation of fast and of abstinence from meat on the prescribed days is suspended."
>
> Since regulars were not mentioned in this indult, the undersigned asks whether they also can make use of it on

[14] *Constitutiones Aloysianae, 1889,* n. 173.

[15] *Constitutiones Generales Fratrum Minorum, 1897,* n. 173.

[16] *Constitutiones Generales Ordinis Fratrum Minorum, 1953,* art. 182; art. 184.

[17] *Constitutiones Fratrum Minorum S. Francisci Capuccinorum, 1909,* n. 68.

[18] *Constitutiones Fratrum Minorum Capuccinorum, 1925,* n. 70.

[19] *Constitutiones Ordinis Fratrum Minorum Sancti Patris Francisci Conventualium, 1932,* n. 320.

Friday and on Saturday, and even during Lent. This question was asked also by Superiors of other convents.

Father Seraphin, Provincial

Wednesday, January 4, 1892.

In a General Congregation of the Supreme Roman and Universal Inquisition, the Most Eminent Lord Cardinal General Inquisitors, with the approval of Our Most Holy Lord, have come to a decision that regarding the foregoing submitted petition the answer should be given that "they are comprehended."

I. Mancini

Notary of the Supreme Roman and Universal Inquisition.[20]

The foregoing response established a principle which may still be followed[21] whenever local ordinaries, in the name of the Holy See, grant a dispensation from the laws of fast and abstinence for reasons of public health. In such cases:

1) The Franciscans may make use of such dispensations with regard to fasts and abstinences imposed either by the law of the Order or by the general law of the Church.

2) They may take advantage of the indults even when they grant

[20] "*Beatissimo Padre,*

Attesa l'Influenza che anche in Parma serpeggia, Monsignor Vescovo pubblicò un indulto concepito nei seguenti termini.

'Finche dura l'Influenza, ossia l'infezione morbosa, che va sempre più diffondendosi, Noi, autorizzati da Roma, dichiariamo sospeso l'obbligo del digiuno e dell'astinenza dalle carni nei giorni prescritti.'

Non essendo nel lodato Indulto nominati i Regolari, il sottoscritto domanda se anch'essi possano farne uso nei giorni di Venerdì, e Sabato, ed anche nella Quaresima. Questa domanda vien fatta anche da più Superiori di altri conventi.

Fr. Serafino, Provinciale

Feria IV, 20 Januarii 1892.

In Congregatione Generali Supremae Romanae et Universalis Inquisitionis, propositis suprascriptis precibus, Emi Dñi Cardinales Generales Inquisitores, adprobante SSmo Domino Nostro, respondendum decreverunt:—*Comprehendi.*

I. Mancini

S. R. et Universalis Inquisitionis Notarius."—*Analecta Ordinis Fratrum Minorum Capuccinorum,* VIII (1892), p. 33; *AOFM,* XI (1892), p. 34.

[21] Canon 4.

a complete dispensation from the law of fast, and not merely when they permit the use of otherwise forbidden foods.

3) They may use the dispensations even when no mention is made of regulars when the indult is given.

An earlier rescript of the Supreme Roman and Universal Inquisition of November 18, 1891, explained the special obligation of Franciscans when a dispensation was given from the law of abstinence on Friday, even when regulars were explicitly included:

> Wednesday, November 18, 1891.
>
> The following doubt was proposed to the Sacred Congregation of the Holy Office, namely: "Whether Franciscan religious may enjoy special indults granted during the year by the Holy See for the eating of meat on Friday, when in such indults there is added the phrase "inclusive of Regulars"?
>
> In a meeting held on Wednesday, November 18, 1891, after giving the matter mature deliberation, the Most Eminent Cardinal Inquisitors General replied:—In the Negative; and they directed that this response be made known to the three Ministers General of the Order of Saint Francis.[22]

The indults considered here are not those which the Holy See grants for reasons of public health. The application of indults of that nature is taken care of by the previously listed reply given on January 4, 1892. They are dispensations from the law of Friday abstinence, which the Holy See may see fit to grant for some other reason. When such dispensations were given, the Franciscans were not permitted to use them because of their special obligation of fast that proceeds from the Rule.

The traditional pre-Code doctrine of what the law of fast implies was the fundamental reason for the decision reached by the Fathers

---

[22] "Feria IV, die 18 Novemb. 1891.

Sequens dubium Sacrae Congregationi S. Officii propositum fuerat, scilicet:—'An Religiosi Franciscales frui possint feria sexta peculiaribus indultis pro esu carnium infra annum a S. Sede concessis, addita clausula: *Regularibus comprehensis?*'

In Congressu feriae IV diei 18 Novembris 1891 re mature perpensa, Em̃i Cardinales Inquisitores Generales responderunt: Negative; et hoc responsum singulis tribus Ministris Generalibus Ordinis S. Francisci notificandum esse statuerunt."—*AOFMC,* VIII (1892), 33; *AOFM,* X (1891), 187.

of the Congregation. Under the older law, the Franciscans were obliged to abstain from meat on Friday, not only in consequence of the universal law of abstinence, but also as part of the obligation of fast imposed by the Rule. In effect, the Friars were bound by a double obligation of abstinence, one from Church law, and the other from the Rule as included in their obligation to observe the fast. When a dispensation was given from the Church law alone, it touched only the obligation stemming from the Church law, and not the special obligation deriving from the Rule. Hence, when the Holy See dispensed the faithful at large from their obligation of Friday abstinence, it in no way affected the obligation which Franciscans had from the Rule.

The fourth and last important reply was the solution given by the Sacred Congregation of Religious, on September 1, 1912, to a number of doubts which had been proposed by the Superior General of the Congregation of the Mission:

> The Most Reverend Lord Anthony Fiat, Superior General of the Congregation of the Mission and of the Daughters of Charity, requested a solution of the following doubt from the Sacred Congregation of Religious, namely:
>
> Whether in Apostolic indults whereby mitigations in and dispensations from abstinence and fast are granted for regions both in and outside of Europe, and especially in Latin America, there are included the Religious Families which dwell in these regions?
>
> The Most Eminent and Most Reverend Fathers Cardinals of this same Congregation, gathered together in the Vatican Palace on the thirtieth day of August, 1912, after putting the matter to mature deliberation, replied:
>
> I. In the Affirmative with regard to abstinence and fast prescribed by the general law of the Church, unless religious are excluded from the indult.
>
> II. In the Negative with regard to abstinence and fast established by their own Rules and Constitutions, unless mention is expressly made of this dispensation in the Indult. Therefore, those who do not observe the abstinence and fast of this sort transgress the Rule and the Constitutions indeed, but not the law of the Church.

Consequently, they incur only the fault and the punishment stated by the Constitutions or by the Rules.

III. With reference, however, to those religious who live in Latin America, the most recent indult granted by the Secretariate of State on January 1, 1910, is to be observed.

Which response of the Most Eminent Lord Cardinals Our Most Holy Lord Pope Pius X deigned to approve and to confirm on September 1, 1912, at the relation of the undersigned Secretary.

All things to the contrary notwithstanding.

Given at Rome from the Secretariate of the Sacred Congregation of Religious, September 1, 1912.

Fr. J. C. Cardinal Vives, Prefect.

✠ Donatus, Archbishop of Ephesus, Secretary[23]

---

[23] "Rm̃us D. Antonius Fiat, Superior generalis Congregationis Missionis et Filiarum a Caritate, a S. C. de Religiosis sequentis dubii solutionem expostulavit, nimirum:

Utrum in indultis apostolicis, quibus mitigationes vel dispensationes conceduntur ab abstinentia et ieiunio in regionibus intra et extra Europam, praesertim in America Latina, comprehendantur Familiae religiosae ibi degentes.

Em̃i autem ac Rm̃i Patres Cardinales sacrae eiusdem Congregationis, in aedibus Vaticanis adunati die 30 augusti 1912, re maturo examine perpensa, responderunt:

I. Affirmative quoad abstinentiam et ieiunium a lege Ecclesiae generali praescripta, nisi ab indulto excludantur religiosi.

II. Negative quoad abstinentiam et ieiunium a propriis Regulis et Constitutionibus statuta, nisi in indulto expresse de hac dispensatione mentio habeatur. Non servantes igitur huiusmodi abstinentiam et ieiunium, transgrediuntur quidem Regulam et Constitutionem, non autem legem Ecclesiae; ideoque culpam tantum et poenam incurrunt a Constitutionibus vel Regulis statutam.

III. Quoad vero Religiosos in America Latina degentes, standum novissimo Indulto per Secretariam Status concesso, die 1 ianuarii an. 1910.

Quas Em̃orum DD. Cardinalium responsiones Ssm̃us Dominus noster Pius Papa X, ad relationem infrascripti Secretarii, die 1 septembris 1912 adprobare et confirmare dignatus est.

Contrariis non obstantibus quibuscumque.

Datum Romae ex Secretaria sacrae Congregationis de Religiosis. die 1 septembris 1912. Fr. I. C. Card. Vives, *Praefectus.*

✠Donatus, Archiep. Ephesinus, *Secretarius.*"—*Acta Apostolicae Sedis,* IV (1912), p. 626–627; *AOFM,* XXXI (1912), p. 320; *AOFMC,* XXVIII (1912), p. 357.

The foregoing reply, even though it was issued only to a single religious Institute, was, according to the teaching of pre-Code canonists, of general obligation for all religious, especially in view of the fact that it was promulgated by being inserted in the Church's official publication, the *Acta Apostolicae Sedis.*[24] It looked to principles that were later incorporated in the Code of Canon Law. Actually, the reply is one of the sources upon which the legislation of canon 1253 is based; its dispositions are substantially the same as those which are contained in canon 620.

The principles which the reply establishes are these:

1) With regard to obligations imposed only by general Church law, religious are comprehended in Apostolic indults which contain mitigations in and dispensations from fast and abstinence, unless they have been excluded.

2) With regard to obligations imposed exclusively by the Rule and the Constitutions, religious are not comprehended in Apostolic indults which contain mitigations in and dispensations from fast and abstinence, unless they have been expressly included.

3) With regard to obligations that are imposed simultaneously by general Church law and by the Rule or the Constitutions, since the two obligations are separable, religious are partially comprehended and partially excluded according to the principles stated under numbers 1) and 2).

Thus, when an indult containing a dispensation from fast is granted for a day when the obligation of fasting is imposed on religious simultaneously by the general Church law and by the special law of their Institute, that dispensation avails for religious in so far as it removes the obligation imposed by the general Church law, but it does not avail for them effectively, since there remains untouched the obligation imposed by the law of the religious Institute.

This conclusion follows from what was said under Number II of the response. There it was stated that those who do not observe the abstinence and fast of this sort transgress the Rule and the Constitutions indeed, but not the law of the Church. The response dealt principally with obligations which were simul-

---

[24] Wernz, *Ius Decretalium,* I, n. 146, IV.

taneously imposed by the general Church law and by the special religious law. It is evident that the response dealt with an obligation deriving from the Rule and the Constitutions. Otherwise there could not have been any transgression of them. At the same time, the response also dealt with a corresponding but distinct obligation arising from the law of the Church. Otherwise there would not have been any point in its stating that the law of the Church is not transgressed. The reason why Church law is not transgressed is that the indult evinces a dispensation from that law. The reason why the Rule and the Constitutions are transgressed is that the indult has no effect upon the legislation which they impose.

Unless he expressly states his will to the contrary, the legislator means to leave intact every obligation imposed by the special law of religious Institutes, whether that obligation be imposed together with an obligation of the general Church law, or whether it be imposed apart from any obligation of the general Church law.[25]

The doctrine as presented in the foregoing response was nothing new or radical at the time. It was completely in keeping with the constant policy of the Holy See to safeguard the integrity of the specific obligations of religious whenever it granted a dispensation from fast or abstinence.[26] In exceptional circumstances, when the Holy See wished to dispense religious from the obligations of their special law, it left no doubt as to its intention, as when it granted such a dispensation to religious dwelling in Latin America in the year 1910, as a part of the general indult concerning fast and abstinence published for the faithful of the region. Number 5 of that indult, which pertains to religious, reads as follows:

> Religious of both sexes who are not bound by a special vow, even if they are members of the Franciscan families, may, with the consent of their Superiors, use the present

[25] Cf. Fidel de Pamplona, *Ayunos de los religiosos después de la promulgación del Código* (Madrid: Instituto San Raimundo de Peñafort, 1953), p. 13.

[26] Mocchegiani, *Iurisprudentia Ecclesiastica,* II, nn. 75–76; *AOFMC,* VIII (1892), 33; *AOFM,* XI (1892), 34; X (1891), 187; *Commentarium Ordinis Fratrum Minorum Conventualium,* XXXVIII (1941), 87–88; *AAS,* III (1911), 363; *Acta Sanctae Sedis,* XL (1907), 469.

indult, even with reference to abstinences and fasts prescribed in their own Rule or Statutes. Nevertheless, Regular Superiors, particularly Provincials and quasi-Provincials, are exhorted to try to refrain from the use of this type of indult within the cloister in so far as they can. Subjects, however, are to stand by the judgment of their Superiors.[27]

A rescript, dated February 1, 1917, from the Sacred Congregation of Religious to the Vicar General of the Friars Minor in Spain, embodies an interpretation of the *Bulla Cruciata*.[28] The force of the rescript was that there reposed a greater burden upon the Friars Minor than upon other religious.[29] Since the rescript is special in character in that it was issued exclusively to the Order of Friars Minor, some authors have held that it is of obligation only for the Order of Friars Minor, and not for the Friars Minor Conventual nor for the Friars Minor Capuchin.[30]

Section 3. Privileges and Favors

During the centuries previous to the promulgation of the Code, the Franciscans received a number of privileges touching on the discipline of fast and abstinence. According to strict law, these

[27] "Religiosi utriusque sexus, speciali voto non obstricti, quamvis sint ex Ordinis Minorum Familiis, de consensu suorum Superiorum uti possunt praesenti indulto, etiam quoad abstinentias et ieiunia in propria regula sive statutis praescripta. Hortandi tamen sunt Superiores Regulares, praesertim Provinciales et quasi-Provinciales, ut pro viribus abstinere curent ab usu huiusmodi indulti intra claustra; subditi vero stent iudicio suorum Superiorum."—*AAS,* II (1910), p. 217, n. 5.

[28] "Bulla Cruciata in Hispania non derogat legi circa dies ieiunii a regula Fratribus Minoribus praescripti. Speciatim vero circa Quadragesimam Ecclesiae, Fratres non recedant a praxi universali Ordinis. Possunt tamen, servatis servandis, etiam in diebus ieiunii regularis uti Indultis Bullae circa abstinentiam vel qualitatem ciborum."—*AAS,* IX (1917), 135.

[29] Ubach, *Compendium Theologiae Moralis* (2 vols., Friburgii Brisgoviae, 1926–1927), I, n. 372; Ferreres, *Compendium Theologiae Moralis* (12. ed., 2 vols., Barcinone, 1923), II, 814, footnote n. 2; *AAS,* VII (1915), 564.

[30] Cf. Victorius ab Appeltern, *Dissertatio de Modo quo Diversa Ieiunia et Abstinentiae a Religiosis Familiis Hodiendum sunt Observanda,* p. 35; Fidel de Pamplona, *Ayunos de los religiosos después de la promulgación del Código,* pp. 13–14, footnote n. 20; Lizaso-Bolzano, *Exposición de la Regla de los Frailes Menores,* p. 82, footnote n. 9.

privileges still remain in force.[31] For practical purposes, however, they have ceased, since most of the benefits which they conferred have been rendered meaningless and useless by the changes introduced into the common law by the Code. Perhaps the only ancient privilege that might have application today is the concession made by Pope Leo X (1513–1521), in accordance with which the Friars Minor Observant who were traveling could transfer to some other day the obligation of fasting when it fell on the day of their journeying.[32] In virtue of the special grant whereby Pope Saint Pius X acknowledged a mutual and common sharing of privileges among the three Franciscan families,[33] this privilege was shared also by the Conventuals and the Capuchins, both of whom may still continue to use it.[34]

Since the year 1904, the Order of Friars Minor has been in possession of a faculty which states that Friars Minor who happen to be outside the convent during a time of fast prescribed by the Rule may, at the table of their host, adapt themselves to his manner and practice.[35] Since this faculty is renewed every five years, it is not strictly of the nature of a permanently granted privilege. Nevertheless, since Pope Saint Pius X granted to the members of the three Franciscan families the common sharing of favors as well as of privileges,[36] this favor too is shared alike by the three Franciscan families. And since the Code did not revoke the future

[31] Canon 4.

[32] "Leo X concessit, quod Fratres Min. Observantes, itinerantes, possint transferre ieiunium diei itinerationis, in alium diem."—Alphonsus de Casarubios-Hieronymus a Sorbo, *Compendium Privilegiorum Fratrum Minorum* (4. ed., Venetiis, 1609), p. 270.

[33] "Nos vero, ut caritatis fraternitatisque vincula, quibus inter se Franciscales trium familiarum continentur, vel arctiora fiant, haec in perpetuum damus et tribuimus: . . . III. Ut indulgentiae, *gratiae,* exemptiones, privilegia omnia quae uni Minorum familiae concessa vel iam sint vel posthac fuerint, ea ipsa ceteris familiis concessa censeantur et sint."—*AAS,* I (1909), 737. (Italics are supplied by the writer.)

[34] Canon 613, § 1; *AAS,* XXX (1938), 73.

[35] "Fratres Minores extra conventum versantes sese hospitantium mensae conformare possunt, tempore ieiunii a Regula praescripti."—Capobianco, *Privilegia et Facultates Ordinis Fratrum Minorum* (editio altera, Salerni: ex Conventu S. M. Angelorum, 1948), n. 357.

[36] *AAS,* I (1909), 737.

sharing in common of favors, but only that of privileges, Conventual Friars and Capuchin Friars may avail themselves of this faculty even today.

Article II. Franciscan Fast and Abstinence and the Code

Section 1. Relationship of the Franciscan Discipline to That of the Code

Although the Code introduced a certain uniformity into the general Church discipline on fast and abstinence, it did it in such a way as to safeguard the special laws of religious Institutes and the provisions of special indults.[37] Since the Franciscans are under no specially added obligation of any kind with regard to their observance of the fasts and the abstinences imposed by the Code on all Christians, they may observe these obligations in exactly the same way as the rest of the faithful. With regard to the fasts and the abstinences imposed by their own special law, however, they are in certain cases bound by special regulations.

Canon 1253 states that the canons on fast and abstinence change nothing of the legislation that is contained in and enacted by the Rules and the Constitutions of religious Institutes. The dispositions of the Franciscan Rule, and also of the Constitutions, correspondingly remain intact. The legislation of the Franciscan Rule on fast and abstinence, however, is very brief. The Rule does no more than to state that certain days are to be kept as days of fast, and that certain seasons are to be kept as "Lents." [38] Hence, with regard to the Franciscan Rule, the implication of canon 1253 is simply that the dispositions of the Code do not abolish either the days of fast or the "Lents."

Although the Rule prescribes certain fasts, it states absolutely nothing about how these fasts are to be observed. If one had only the Rule as his law of fasting, he would know that he had an obligation to fast, and he would know when he was bound to fulfill that obligation, but he would not know how to go about fulfilling it.

This deficiency in the Rule is not an oversight. It is not a mistake. On the contrary, it is a manifestation of the wisdom and

[37] Cf. Canons 4; 22; 1253.

[38] *Opuscula Sancti Patris Francisci*, p. 66.

the foresight of Saint Francis, the Rule's author. Francis was brief and to the point in prescribing for the Friars their obligation of fasting. He was precise in indicating exactly when they were bound to fast. But he realized that changing circumstances would make it inadvisable and imprudent for him to legislate further on exactly how the obligation was to be fulfilled. He left to the general Church law all secondary modifications of the Rule's precept regarding the fast.

Thus, at one time, the law of the Church forbade the eating of meat, of eggs, and of milk products during a time of fast. Later, it forbade the eating of meat and of fish at the same meal on a fast day.[39] At the time when these laws were in force, Franciscans too were bound to their observance, even during times of fast prescribed by the Rule.

On the other hand, at no time in the history of the Order did the Church demand fasting on a Sunday. Consequently, Franciscans were never bound to fast on Sundays, either during times of fasts imposed by the Rule or during the seasons of fasting imposed by the Church.[40] The Friars have always observed the discipline of fasting according to the modifications that the law of the time placed upon it.

Now, as formerly, the Franciscans have to look to the general law of the Church to discover just how they must go about fulfilling the obligation of fast imposed by the Rule. The present Constitutions furnish some guidance in the matter, but they do not provide for every case.

The Constitutions of all three Franciscan families permit the Friars to conform to local usage with regard to the quantity and the quality of the foods permitted on a day of fast.[41] In all the

---

[39] Wernz-Vidal, *Ius Canonicum,* IV, n. 524.

[40] Fidel de Pamplona, "Ayunos y Abstinencias en la Regla Franciscana," *IS,* I (1955), 285.

[41] *Constitutiones Generales Ordinis Fratrum Minorum,* 1953, Art. 182, § 1: "Lex ieiunii secundum ius commune, praeter unicam comestionem seu prandium, permittit aliquid cibi sumere mane et vespere, servata tamen circa ciborum quantitatem et qualitatem consuetudine locorum, in quibus actu religiosi commorantur." Art. 184, § 1: "Religiosi Ordinis nostri, quod ad qualitatem ciborum attinet, diebus ieiunii a S. Regula impositi, indultis ab Ordinario loci nomine S. Sedis publicatis uti possunt."

fasts and the abstinences prescribed by the Rule or by their respective Constitutions, the Friars Minor and the Friars Minor Capuchin may follow the dispositions of the Code with regard to the age at which the obligation of fasting begins or also ends. Conventual Friars, however, must follow the special norm prescribed by their Constitutions in these fasts and abstinences.[42]

The Constitutions of the Conventual Friars incorporate the norm of canon 1252, § 4, which states that the Friars need never fast either on Sundays or on feastdays of precept outside of Lent, nor need they anticipate vigils.[43] This modality of fasting is not found in the Constitutions of either the Friars Minor or the Friars Minor Capuchin. Nevertheless, since the Friars of both these latter branches of the Order are in need of some practical norm to follow in these circumstances, they may make use of these prescriptions of canon 1252, § 4. Capuchins may follow this norm with regard to the Sundays, the feast days of precept, and the vigils. Friars Minor, however, by reason of a particular response which they received from the Holy See, dated March 22, 1921,[44]

Constitutiones Ordinis Fratrum Minorum Sancti Patris Francisci Conventualium, 1932, n. 320: "Diebus ieiunii et abstinentiae nec non solius ieiunii, praeter unicam per diem comestionem, licet aliquid cibi mane et vespere sumere, servata tamen circa ciborum quantitatem et qualitatem probata locorum consuetudine."

Constitutiones Fratrum Minorum Capuccinorum, 1925, n. 70: "Tempore vero et diebus quibus fratres, etiam ex Regulae praecepto, ieiunare tenentur, quoad qualitatem et quantitatem ciborum, legibus Ecclesiae vel specialibus Sanctae Sedis indultis concessis pro regionibus ubi degunt, aut probatis locorum consuetudinibus se conformare possunt."

[42] *Constitutiones Ordinis Fratrum Minorum Sancti Patris Francisci Conventualium, 1932,* n. 323: "Ad ieiunii et abstinentiae, quae a Regula et Constitutionibus praescribuntur, observationem omnes et singuli fratres professi, cuiuscumque aetatis et conditionis sint, omnino adstringuntur."

[43] *Constitutiones Ordinis Fratrum Minorum Sancti Patris Francisci Conventualium, 1932,* n. 321.

[44] "Quum a pluribus, fratribus, post promulgatum Codicem I. C. proposita fuisset quaestio, utrum servandum sit ieiunium Regulae die festo Immaculatae Conceptionis B. M. et generatim quando festum de praecepto occurrit aliqua sexta feria, aliis aliud opinantibus, Definitorium Generale censuit expedire, ut ab ipsa S. Sede per Procuratorum Generalem Ordinis expeteretur solutio dubii.

may not follow the norm of the canon with regard to feast days of precept, although they may do so with regard to Sundays and vigils. The Friars of all three branches, however, may make use of the concession granted in canon 1251, § 2, which permits the eating of meat and of fish at the same meal, as well as the interchange of the main meal with the collation on a fast day.

Since the Code likewise preserves the force of past indults, according to the terms of the rescript issued to the Franciscan Minister Provincial of Bologna on January 20, 1892, the Friars may still take advantage of dispensations, even from fasts imposed in the Rule, when they are granted by Apostolic authority for reasons of public health.[45]

Section 2. Dispensations from Local Ordinaries According to the Code

The dispensatory power with which the Code of Canon Law vests local ordinaries with regard to the obligations of religious is found in Canon 620. There it is stated that, in virtue of an indult lawfully granted by a local ordinary, an obligation of the common law ceases also for all religious living in the diocese, without

---

S. C. de Religiosis autem die 22 martii misit ad Procuratorem Generalem epistolam quae sequitur:

Revm̃e Pater,

Haec S. Congregatio, mature perpenso dubio exposito 'Utrum diebus festis de praecepto extra Quadragesimam cesset lex ieiunii, quae continetur in Regula Fratrum Minorum,' atque attentis omnibus ad rem facientibus, rescribendum censuit prout rescribit: 'Negative.'

Haec a me communicanda erant cum P. T., cui fausta omnia adpraecor a Domino, atque permaneo.

Addictissimus

Maurus M. Serafini, Ab. O. S. B.
Secretarius."

—*AOFM*, XL (1921), 125; *AOFMC*, XXXVII (1921), 157.

The Capuchin Definitory General, in a declaration of March 6, 1931, stated that, according to the norm of the reply of the Sacred Congregation of Religious of March 22, 1921, it cannot be deduced from n. 70 of the Capuchin Constitutions that the precept of fasting sometimes ceases for our Friars on days of fast prescribed by the Rule.—*AOFMC*, XLVII (1931), 86.

[45] Canon 4; *AOFM*, XI (1892), 34; *AOFMC*, VIII (1892), 33.

prejudice to their vows and to the proper Constitutions of their Institute.[46] The principles invoked in the canon make it clear to just what extent the Franciscans may make use of episcopal indults which relax the obligation of fast and abstinence.

1) An indult which when granted by a local ordinary dispenses from fast and abstinence does not avail for the Franciscans with regard to obligations which arise exclusively from the law of the Order. The canon plainly speaks of an indult in virtue of which *an obligation of the common law ceases.*[47] Obligations arising from a special law, therefore, are completely outside of its scope.

2) An indult which when granted by a local ordinary dispenses from fast and abstinence avails for the Franciscans with regard to obligations which arise exclusively from the law of the Church. It is principally these obligations that canon 620 contemplates when it deals with an indult in virtue of which *an obligation of the common law ceases.*[48]

3) An indult which when granted by a local ordinary dispenses from fast and abstinence avails partially for the Franciscans with regard to obligations which arise simultaneously from the law of the Order and the law of the Church. It avails for them in that it removes that part of the obligation which is imposed by the common law. It does not avail for them effectively with respect to what is imposed by the law of the Order.

The canon makes provision for the case wherein a double obligation is involved when it adds the clause, *without prejudice to their vows and to the proper Constitutions of their Institute.*[49] The legislator wishes to grant to religious the benefit of his dispensation from the common law, but he also wishes to leave untouched the obligation imposed by the special law of their Institute, even when that obligation is imposed simultaneously with the obligation that derives from the common law.

The canon is concerned with safeguarding the vows of the

[46] "Per indultum ab Ordinario loci legitime concessum, obligatio legis communis cessat quoque pro religiosis omnibus in dioecesi commorantibus, salvis votis et constitutionibus propriis cuiusvis religionis."—Canon 620.

[47] ". . . obligatio legis communis cessat."

[48] ". . . obligatio legis communis cessat."

[49] ". . . salvis votis et constitutionibus propriis cuiusvis religionis."

religious and the Constitutions of their religious Institutes. It states nothing explicitly about the Rules of these Institutes. Nevertheless, the canon is not to be thought of as excluding these latter. It employs the term *Constitutions,* not in the very specific sense in which it is used in the Franciscan Order, but in a somewhat broader sense, so as to include all special law of a religious Institute.[50]

Absolutely, then, the clause, *without prejudice to their vows and to the proper Constitutions of their Institute,*[51] may be interpreted to mean simply that religious may not make use of a dispensation from the common law if they are forbidden to do so either by vow or by the special law of their Institute. It is conceivable that such special law may contain a prohibition of that sort. But it is not conceivable that religious would make such a prohibition the object of a vow. What the canon is referring to when it treats of vows is the vow of perpetual abstinence taken by certain religious. It is the common practice of the Holy See to except the obligation imposed on religious by such vows from the effect of dispensations contained in indults concerning fast and abstinence.[52]

In keeping with the same principle upon which canon 620 is based, namely that the privilege of exemption should not become a burden to those who enjoy it,[53] pastors too may validly dispense Franciscan Friars residing within their parishes from the obligation of the fasts and the abstinences imposed by the common law according to the prescriptions of canon 1245, § 1.

Since the Franciscan Rule simply calls to mind the Church-imposed obligation of observing the Lent preceding Easter,[54] the Friars are bound only by the common law to that observance.

---

[50] Matthaeus Conte a Coronata, *Institutiones,* I, n. 627.

[51] ". . . salvis votis et constitutionibus propriis cuiusvis religionis."

[52] Cf. *AOFM,* XI (1892), 66; *AOFM,* XX (1901), 202–203; *ASS,* XL (1907), 469; *AAS,* II (1910), 217, n. 5; *AAS,* III (1911), 363; *AAS,* VII (1915), 555; *AAS,* VII (1915), 564; *AAS,* IX (1917), 84; Albertus a Bulsano, *Expositio Regulae FF. Minorum, 1932,* pp. 251–252; Mocchegiani, *Iurisprudentia Ecclesiastica,* II, nn. 75–76.

[53] "Quod ob gratiam alicuius conceditur non est in eius dispendium retorquendum."—Reg. 61, R. J., in VI°; Matthaeus Conte a Coronata, *Institutiones,* I, n. 627.

[54] See Chapter I, Article V, *supra.*

Hence, according to the prescriptions of canon 620, when a local ordinary dispenses from the Lenten fast, the Franciscans may avail themselves of that dispensation. Nevertheless, there can be cases wherein an obligation of fasting as imposed by the Rule will coincide with a similar obligation imposed by the common law. For example, on an Ember Friday a Franciscan is bound to the fasting precept by way of such a double obligation. If a local ordinary dispenses from the Ember Friday fast, in keeping with what is prescribed in canon 620, then a Franciscan is still bound to observe the fast by reason of the precept contained in the Rule.

Authors are in error if they teach that when, as on Ember Fridays, an obligation of fasting as imposed by the Rule coincides with a similar obligation deriving from the common law, the obligation rooted in the Rule ceases automatically upon the granting of a dispensation from the obligation deriving from the common law.[55]

Intrinsically, the two precepts of the fast on Ember Friday, that of the Rule and that of the common law, are identical. They are materially identical, for they both set up the same obligation, namely that of fasting; and they both impose this obligation on the same day. They are formally identical, for they both have the same intrinsic formal object, namely the virtue of temperance. Extrinsically, however, the two precepts are formally distinct, in as much as they pertain to formally distinct bodies of laws. The precept of fasting on an Ember Friday is part of the common law of the Church, the formal object of which is Christian perfection in general. The precept of fasting on all Fridays is part of the special law of the Franciscan Order, the formal object of which is specifically Franciscan perfection.

As part of his responsibility of leading the faithful to Christian perfection, the local ordinary possesses a certain authority over the common law, and he has the power to dispense from various obligations which that law imposes, such as the obligation to fast on Ember Friday. Since the Franciscans have been withdrawn from

[55] Cf. Albertus a Bulsano, *Expositio Regulae FF. Minorum, 1932,* n. 168; Victorius ab Appeltern, *Dissertatio de Modo quo Diversa Ieiunia et Abstinentiae a Religiosis Familiis Hodiendum sunt Observanda,* p. 12; Mocchegiani, *Iurisprudentia Ecclesiastica,* II, n. 76. The doctrine of these three authors manifests this erroneous outlook.

the jurisdiction of the local ordinary, however, in all matters which pertain to the attainment of the specific perfection of their special state, the local ordinary has no authority to dispense them from those obligations which are imposed by the special law of the Order and which are specifically ordained to Franciscan perfection. Extrinsically, therefore, a dispensation granted by the local ordinary from the Ember Friday fast can have no effect upon the special obligation of fasting on all Fridays which is imposed by the Franciscan Rule.

Intrinsically too, a local ordinary's dispensation from the Ember Friday fast leaves intact the obligation of the Friday fast as prescribed in the Franciscan Rule. An obligation ceases intrinsically by reason of the cessation of its intrinsic formal object. The effect of the local ordinary's dispensation, however, is not directed to the intrinsic formal object of the obligation of fasting. The dispensation does not bring about the cessation of that object.[56] The intrinsic formal object of the fast remains in existence even after the dispensation has been granted, but its attainment is no longer imposed as binding. The effect of the local ordinary's dispensation is rather directed toward the *obligation* of the law of fasting. When a local ordinary dispenses from the fast on Ember Friday, the faithful are relieved of their *obligation* to fast. They are no longer bound to strive for the intrinsic formal object of the obligation of fasting, namely the virtue of temperance, although that object remains intact. The intrinsic formal object, which is common to the obligation of the Ember Friday fast and to the Friday fast of the Franciscan Rule, therefore, continues to be imposed by the Rule in an obligatory manner upon Franciscans, even though the obligation of the Ember Friday fast has ceased to bind in consequence of the dispensation granted by the local ordinary.

Intrinsically, therefore, as well as extrinsically, an obligation of fasting imposed by the Franciscan Rule which coincides with a like obligation imposed by the common law always continues to bind, even after a dispensation has been conceded by the local ordinary

[56] Fidel de Pamplona, *Ayunos de los religiosos después de la promulgación del Código,* p. 12.

from the common law fast. The Friars are bound to keep such fasts, no longer by reason of the common law, but by reason of the precept imposed by the Rule.

Article III. Dispensations Granted by Local Ordinaries According to Special Faculties

The extraordinary conditions brought about by the second World War moved the Holy See, on December 19, 1941, to empower local ordinaries with special broad faculties for dispensing from fast and abstinence. The text of the decree follows:

> In view of the peculiar circumstances of the present time, His Holiness, Pius XII, by Divine Providence Pope, has graciously deigned to grant to all Ordinaries of places, of whatever rite, the faculty to give according to their prudent discretion, within the territory of their jurisdiction, a general dispensation from the law of ecclesiastical fast and abstinence, in favor also of religious men and women who enjoy the privilege of exemption.
>
> Nevertheless the law of ecclesiastical fast and abstinence is to remain binding, for the faithful of the Latin rite, on Ash Wednesday and Good Friday, and for the faithful of other rites on two days to be determined by their Ordinaries.
>
> The Ordinaries of places who grant the above dispensation should, however, exhort all the faithful, especially the secular and regular clergy and communities of religious women, that they make compensation in some way for the favors thus granted, by voluntary practices of Christian mortification and expiation, by applying themselves to good works, especially toward the sick and the poor, and by pouring forth fervent prayers to God according to the intention of the Supreme Pontiff.
>
> All things to the contrary notwithstanding.
>
> From the Vatican, 19 Dec., 1941.[57]

---

[57] Bouscaren, *The Canon Law Digest* (3 vols., Milwaukee: The Bruce Publishing Company, 1934–1954), II, 363 (hereafter cited as *Digest*).

S. C. pro Negotiis Ecclesiasticis Extraordinariis, indultum, 19 dec. 1941:

Attentis peculiaribus hodiernis rerum adiunctis, Ssmus Dominus Noster Pius Divina Providentia PP. XII omnibus Ordinariis locorum, cuiuslibet ritus, quamdiu praesens bellum perdurabit, benigne concedere dignatus est, ut, pro suo prudenti arbitrio, in territorio suae iurisdictionis, indulgeant generalem dispensationem super lege abstinentiae et ieiunii ecclesiastici, in

On January 22, 1946, the Holy See extended these faculties indefinitely:

> In view of the difficult conditions following the recent war, His Holiness by Divine Providence Pope Pius XII has graciously deigned to extend on the same terms, until other provision is made, the Apostolic Indult of 19 Dec., 1941, regarding the law of ecclesiastical abstinence and fasting.
>
> Accordingly all Ordinaries of places of whatever rite can grant, according to their prudent judgment, in the territory of their respective jurisdictions, a general dispensation from the law of ecclesiastical abstinence and fast, in favor also of religious men and women, even those who enjoy the privilege of exemption.
>
> But the law of ecclesiastical abstinence and fast remains in effect, for the faithful of the Latin rite, on Ash Wednesday and Good Friday; for the faithful of other rites, on two days to be determined by their respective Ordinaries.
>
> Local Ordinaries who grant the above dispensation shall take care to exhort the faithful, especially the secular clergy and religious men and women, to try to compensate for this favor by voluntary practices of Christian perfection and expiation and by good works, especially of charity toward the poor and the sick; and let them not fail to offer pious prayers to God according to the intention of the same Holy Father.
>
> Rome, the 22nd of January, 1946.[58]

---

favorem etiam religiosorum et religiosarum exemptionis privilegio utentium.

Firma tamen maneat lex abstinentiae et ecclesiastici ieiunii, pro fidelibus ritus latini, Feria IV Cinerum et Feria VI in Parasceve, pro fidelibus vero alius ritus duobus diebus ab eorum Ordinariis statuendis.

Ordinarii autem locorum, qui supradictam dispensationem concedunt, fideles omnes hortentur, praesertim vero Clerum saecularem ac regularem necnon sacrarum Virginum familias, ut ii christianae mortificationis et expiationis voluntariis exercitiis, bonis operibus potissimum erga aegros ac inopes vacantes, et ad mentem Summi Pontificis fervidas Deo preces fundentes, aliquo modo indulti facilitates compensare valeant.

Contrariis quibuslibet non obstantibus.

Ex Aedibus Vaticanis, die 19 mensis Decembris a. 1941.

A. Card. Maglione, *a Secretis Status*

S. Congr. pro Negotiis Ecclesiasticis Extraordinariis Praefectus"—*AAS*, XXXIII (1941), 516–517.

[58] Bouscaren, *Digest*, III, 493–494.

The faculties were again extended on January 28, 1949, when in view of somewhat improved conditions certain modifications were introduced:

> A Decree of the S. C. of the Council on the observance of the law of abstinence and fast, is as follows:
>
> Since the adverse circumstances which counseled the relaxation, in December, 1941, of the law of abstinence and fast, have nearly everywhere somewhat improved, it has been decided, at the approach of the propitious time of the Holy Year and at the request of a number of Most Excellent Ordinaries, to restore the law at least in part.
>
> Accordingly His Holiness Pius XII by divine Providence Pope has deigned to decree for all the faithful of the Latin rite, including those who belong to religious orders and congregations, to limit the faculty granted to Ordinaries to dispense from the aforesaid law, so that, from the first day of the coming Lent and until some different provision is made, the law of abstinence is to be

---

S. C. C., indultum, 22 ian. 1946:

"Attentis difficilibus rerum adiunctis quae recens bellum sequuta sunt. Ssmus Dominus Noster Pius Divina Providentia Pp. XII benigne prorogare dignatus est, in iisdem terminis et donec aliter provideatur, Apostolicum Indultum diei 19 Decembris 1941 circa legem abstinentiae et ieiunii ecclesiastici.

Quapropter omnes locorum Ordinarii, cuiuslibet ritus, concedere poterunt, secundum prudens ipsorum iudicium, in territorio propriae iurisdictionis, generalem dispensationem super lege abstinentiae et ieiunii ecclesiastici, in favorem quoque Religiosorum et Religiosarum etiam exemptionis privilegio fruentium.

Firma tamen manet lex abstinentiae et ieiunii ecclesiastici, pro fidelibus ritus latini, Feria IV Cinerum et Feria VI in Parasceve; pro fidelibus vero alius ritus, duobus diebus ab eorum Ordinariis statuendis.

Locorum autem Ordinarii, qui supra memoratam dispensationem concessuri sunt, hortari curabunt fideles, praesertim Clerum saecularem, Religiosos ac Religiosas, ut hanc apostolicam concessionem compensare studeant voluntariis exercitiis christianae perfectionis et expiationis atque bonis operibus, praecipue caritatis erga inopes et aegrotos, neve omittant pias Deo ad mentem eiusdem Pontificis preces offerre.

Romae, die 22 Ianuarii an. 1946.

F. Card. Marmaggi, *Praefectus*
Sacrae Congregationis Concilii
I. Bruno, *Secretarius*."—

AAS, XXXVIII, (1946), 27.

observed on all Fridays; and the law of abstinence and fast together is to be observed on Ash Wednesday, Good Friday, and the vigils of the Assumption of Our Lady and of the Nativity of Our Lord; graciously providing, however, that it is allowed everywhere to take eggs and milk products even in the morning and even on days of abstinence and fast together.

Local Ordinaries who make use of this new faculty to dispense from the law of abstinence and fast shall not fail to exhort the faithful, especially clerics and religious men and women, in view of the critical circumstances of the present time, to be generous in performing additional voluntary works of Christian perfection and of charity especially toward the poor and the sick, and also to pray for the intentions of the Holy Father.

Given at Rome, the 28th of January, 1949.[59]

The foregoing concessions to local ordinaries brought about a sweeping change in the law concerning their power to grant general

[59] Bouscaren, *Digest,* III, 494–495.

S. C. C., decr. 28 ian. 1949:

"Cum adversa rerum adiuncta, quae legem abstinentiae et ieiunii mense Decembri a. D. 1941 relaxandam suaserunt, fere ubique aliquantum remissa sint, adveniente propitio Anni Sancti tempore, pluribus postulantibus Excellentissimis Ordinariis, visum est ut saltem ex parte lex ipsa restauretur.

Quapropter Ssmus Dominus Noster Pius divina Providentia Pp. XII decernere dignatus est pro omnibus fidelibus ritus latini, etiam pertinentibus ad Ordines et Congregationes Religiosas, facultatem Ordinariis concessam super praedictam legem dispensandi ita coarctari ut, a prima die proximae Sacrae Quadragesimae et donec aliter provideatur, abstinentia servetur singulis feriis sextis; lex vero abstinentiae simul et ieiunii feria quarta Cinerum, feria sexta Maioris Hebdomadae, pervigiliis Assumptionis B. M. V. et Nativitatis D. N. I. C.; benigne tamen indulgens ut diebus abstinentiae simul et ieiunii ova et lacticinia etiam mane et vespere ubique sumere liceat.

Locorum autem Ordinarii, qui nova hac legis abstinentiae et ieiunii moderatione utuntur, fideles hortari ne omittant, praesertim clericos, religiosos et religiosas, ut gravissimis hisce temporibus voluntaria christianae perfectionis exercitia nec non caritatis opera, maxime erga inopes et aegrotos, libenter addant, itemque ad mentem Summi Pontificis preces effundant.

Datum Romae, die 28 Ianuarii 1949.

F. Card. Marmaggi, *Praefectus*
Sacrae Congregationis Concilii
F. Roberti, *a secretis.*"—

AAS, XLI (1949), 32–33.

dispensations from fast and abstinence. For all practical purposes, these special faculties set aside the legislation of the Code on the matter. According to canon 1245, § 2, local ordinaries may dispense in a general way from fast and abstinence by reason of a great gathering of people, or by reason of the demands of public health. On the other hand, according to the special faculties granted in 1949, local ordinaries may always dispense in a general way from fast and abstinence, with but two restrictions:—1) the law of abstinence is to be observed on all Fridays; and 2) the law of abstinence and fast together is to be observed on Ash Wednesday, on Good Friday, and on the vigils of the Assumption and of Christmas.

The explicit manner in which they treat of the fasts and abstinences of religious makes it clear that the special faculties concede something more to local ordinaries with regard to these obligations than is conceded by the Code. Unless the faculties were granting greater powers than are granted by canon 620, there would be no purpose to their stating that even exempt religious are included, for, according to canon 620, all religious may profit by dispensations from the common law given by local ordinaries. Furthermore, when they treat of religious, the faculties omit the clause of canon 620, *without prejudice to their vows and to the proper Constitutions of their Institute.*[60] Evidently, the faculties empower local ordinaries to dispense from fast and abstinence in favor of religious, even when that dispensation affects obligations arising from the special law of their Institutes.[61]

While it was clear that the special faculties, according to the formula of 1941, granted to local ordinaries powers broader than those granted by the Code for dispensing from the obligations of religious, the precise extent of those powers was not so apparent. It was for this reason that Cardinal Segura, Archbishop of Seville, had recourse to the Holy See for a clarification of the uncertainty. The Cardinal's petition was concerned with fasts and abstinences which arose exclusively from the special law of religious. If these obligations were included in the local ordinaries' special

[60] ". . . salvis votis et constitutionibus propriis cuiusvis religionis."

[61] Fidel de Pamplona, *Ayunos de los religiosos después de la promulgación del Código,* pp. 16–17.

faculties, then mixed obligations, imposed simultaneously by the common law and the special religious law, would also be included. A summary of Cardinal Segura's petition and the reply which he received follow:

> "Pius XII, by means of the Sacred Congregation for Extraordinary Affairs, granted to local ordinaries of whatever rite, for as long as the present war lasts, the faculty to dispense from fast and abstinence in a general way, even in favor of exempt men and women religious to the exception for the faithful of the Latin rite of the abstinence and the fast of Ash Wednesday, and for the faithful of other rites two days determined by their ordinary.
>
> When doubts arose concerning the extent of this concession with regard to those religious Orders and Congregations which have special days of fast and of abstinence prescribed by their Constitutions, Rules, Usages, and Customs, which are different from those prescribed by the Code of Canon Law, the Most Eminent Lord Cardinal Segura, Archbishop of Seville, had recourse, by means of the Nunciature, to the Most Eminent Lord Cardinal Secretary of State to His Holiness, Prefect of that Sacred Congregation, who replied:
>
> 'The faculty granted in the foregoing indult for the dispensation from fast and abstinence comprehends also particular cases established in the Constitutions of religious Orders, provided that there is no special vow in question.'
>
> Seville, March 19, 1942." [62]

---

[62] "Pío XII, por medio de la S. Cong. de Asuntos Extraordinarios, 19 dic. 1941, concedió a los Ordinarios locales de cualquier rito, mientras dure la guerra actual, facultad de dispensar de un modo general del ayuno y abstinencia, aun en favor de los religiosos y religiosas exentos; exceptuando para los fieles de rito latino la abstinencia y ayuno del Miércoles de Ceniza y Viernes Santo; y para los de otros ritos, dos días determinados por su Ordinario.

Habiéndose suscitado dudas sobre el alcance de esta concesión por lo tocante a aquellas órdenes y congregaciones religiosas que por sus constituciones, reglas, usos y costumbres tuvieron prescritos especiales días de ayuno y abstinencia, diversos de los prescritos en el Código Canónico, el Eminentísimo Señor Cardenal Segura, Arbobispo de Sevilla, recurrió por medio de la Nunciatura al Emmo. Sr. Cardenal Secretario de Estado de Su Santidad, Prefecto de aquella S. Congregación, el cual respondió:

The reply given to Cardinal Segura refers to *Constitutions*, omitting all reference to the other sources of obligation mentioned in the petition. However, the word *Constitutions* in this instance must be taken in the same sense in which it is used in canon 620. It must be understood in general as referring to the special law of religious Institutes,[63] and not merely to Constitutions as they are known in the Franciscan Order. For the Franciscans, therefore, it must be understood to include the obligation of fasts and abstinences imposed either by the Rule or by the Constitutions.

From the foregoing response it is clear that, in virtue of the special faculties which they possess, local ordinaries may validly dispense from the obligation of all fasts and abstinences imposed by the special law of the Franciscan Order.[64] A question may arise, however, concerning the intention of the local ordinary who gives the dispensation. Although he has the power to dispense Franciscans from the fasts and abstinences of their Rule and Constitutions, he may refrain from using that power when he grants a dispensation to the faithful in general.

If the local ordinary does not expressly declare his intention, as may well be the case, recourse must be had to presumptions. The case is not the same as when the Holy See grants a dispensation from fast and abstinence to the faithful in general, because the Holy See has explicitly declared that religious are not comprehended in such dispensations with regard to their special obligations, unless the dispensation expressly includes mention of them.[65] On the other hand, the Holy See has granted the above noted special faculties to local ordinaries in view of extraordinary circumstances. It has included the special obligations of religious

'La facultad concedida en el referido Decreto para la dispensa del ayuno y abstinencia comprende también los casos particulares establecidos en las constituciones de las órdenes religiosas, siempre que no se trate de un voto especial.'

Sevilla, 19 mar. 1942."—

Fidel de Pamplona, *Ayunos de los religiosos después de la promulgación del Código*, pp. 17–18.

[63] Fidel de Pamplona, *Ayunos de los religiosos después de la promulgación del Código*, pp. 18–19.

[64] Regatillo, *Institutiones Iuris Canonici* (4. ed., 2 vols., Santander: Sal Terrae, 1951), II, n. 88.

[65] *AAS*, II (1910), p. 217, n. 5.

within the scope of the faculties, since it does not want religious to be deprived of their benefit. A local ordinary, therefore, when he grants a dispensation in virtue of these special faculties is presumed to have the same intention. Unless he manifests his will to the contrary, he is presumed to have included also the obligations of religious within the terms of his dispensation. He is presumed to have used the faculties exactly as they have been issued to him, and to their fullest extent.

Certain major Superiors within the Franciscan Order may forbid their subjects to make use of dispensations from the Rule and Constitutions granted by local ordinaries in virtue of these special faculties. The effect of such a prohibition, however, would not be to reimpose the obligations as they originally stood. The prohibition would rather be a precept of obedience, dependent for its force upon the authority and the intention of those major Superiors.[66]

Although the reply given to Cardinal Segura is particular in the sense of canon 17, § 3, it is nevertheless an authentic interpretation of the faculties which are enjoyed by all local ordinaries in common. Hence, while the reply imposes no obligation on others, it provides a safe norm of interpretation for all who come into juridic contact with the faculties,[67] both for local ordinaries, who are in possession of the faculties, and for religious, who dwell within the territories of these ordinaries.

Since the faculties issued in 1946 and also the ones issued in 1949 are simply an extension and a modification of the original faculties of 1941, the norms of the rescript given to Cardinal Segura as an authentic interpretation of the original faculties apply equally to the two later grants.

Article IV. Dispensations from Superiors Within the Franciscan Order

The obligation of fast and abstinence in the Franciscan Order

[66] *AOFM,* LXX (1951), 423; Vermeersch-Creusen, *Epitome Iuris Canonici* (3 vols., Vol. I, 7. ed., Romae: Dessain, 1949), n. 780.

[67] Michiels, *Normae Generales Juris Canonici* (editio altera, 2 vols., Romae: Desclée, 1949), I, 512; Jone, *Commentarium in Codicem Iuris Canonici,* I, 36; Regatillo, *Institutiones Iuris Canonici,* I, n. 91,

can arise either from the common law or from the special law of the Order. Franciscan Superiors, although their faculties are not the same in all cases, have the power of dispensing from this obligation, no matter what its source. This present article will treat first of their power of dispensing from the fasts and the abstinences prescribed in the common law, and then of their power of dispensing from the fasts and the abstinences prescribed in the special law of the Order. This latter treatment will be subdivided into a discussion of their power of dispensing from the obligation of fasts and abstinences of the Order according to their ordinary faculties, and a discussion of that power according to the special faculties which they have enjoyed since 1941.

Section 1. Dispensations from the Common Law

Canon 1245, § 3, provides the ordinary norm according to which Superiors in the Franciscan Order may dispense from fasts and abstinences prescribed in the common law. That canon gives Superiors the power of dispensing from these obligations after the manner of pastors. Since pastors may, in individual cases and for a justifying reason, dispense individual persons and individual families subject to them,[68] Franciscan Superiors have the power to dispense their individual subjects in the same manner. Since pastors may dispense individual families as well as individual persons, canonists have tried to accommodate this power also for religious Superiors in some way. Some have taught that Superiors may dispense a minor part of their community as the equivalent of a family.[69] Others have taught that they may dispense an entire community.[70] In any case, if the cause for the dispensation is verified in every subject, a Superior may dispense an entire group, no matter how large, or an entire community, by way of a single act. Thus, for example, a Minister Provincial may dispense a large number of Friars in the theology house of his province,

[68] Canon 1245, § 1.

[69] Matthaeus Conte a Coronata, *Institutiones,* II, n. 821; Vermeersch-Creusen, *Epitome Iuris Canonici,* II, n. 556; Jone, *Commentarium in Codicem Iuris Canonici,* II, 440.

[70] Regatillo, *Institutiones Iuris Canonici,* II, n. 88. See also Bernardino da Sienna, *Esposizione della Regola Francescana,* n. 370.

professors and students, from the Lenten fast, when he knows that the nature and the amount of work which these Friars are called upon to do furnishes a reasonable cause for a dispensation in favor of every individual. Such a dispensation, even though it is granted by way of a single act to a very large group, remains individual, for it looks to the cause for the dispensation in every individual subject.[71]

The power of Franciscan Superiors for dispensing from the fasts and abstinences of the common law extends not only to the Friars who are their own subjects, but also to the visiting Friars who are staying only temporarily,[72] and to persons living night and day in the house as servants, pupils, guests, or patients.[73]

Section 2. Dispensations from the Rule and the Constitutions According to the Ordinary Faculties of Superiors

The Constitutions of the Order of Friars Minor establish detailed norms according to which Superiors may dispense from the fasts and the abstinences imposed by the Rule and by the Constitutions. All Superiors are given the authority to dispense from these obligations in individual cases and for a just cause.[74] The Minister General with his Definitory may dispense an entire province.[75] A Minister Provincial with his Definitory may dispense an individual friary.[76] Ministers Provincial and local Superiors may dispense their respective subjects anywhere.[77] A

---

[71] Vermeersch-Creusen, *Epitome Iuris Canonici,* II, n. 556; Beste, *Introductio in Codicem* (editio altera, Collegeville, Minn.: St. John's Abbey Press, 1944), p. 606.

[72] Vermeersch-Creusen, *Epitome Iuris Canonici,* II, n. 556; Bouscaren-Ellis, *Canon Law* (2. ed., Milwaukee: The Bruce Publishing Company, 1951), p. 691.

[73] Canon 514, § 1.

[74] *Constitutiones Generales Ordinis Fratrum Minorum, 1953,* art. 183.

[75] *Constitutiones Generales Ordinis Fratrum Minorum, 1953,* art. 4, § 2; art. 4, § 3.

[76] *Constitutiones Generales Ordinis Fratrum Minorum, 1953,* art. 4, § 2; art. 4, § 3.

[77] *Constitutiones Generales Ordinis Fratrum Minorum, 1953,* art. 4, § 1, n. 2; art. 4, § 1, n. 3; art. 4, § 3.

Minister Provincial may dispense members of another province who are staying in his province,[78] while a local Superior may dispense members of another friary who happen to be in his district.[79]

The Constitutions of the Order of Friars Minor Conventual are not so detailed in their dispositions. They state merely that, in individual cases and for a just cause, Superiors may dispense their respective subjects from the obligations of the fast, or of abstinence, or of both together, as imposed by the Rule.[80]

The Constitutions of the Order of Friars Minor Capuchin provide no norm according to which Superiors may dispense from the fasts and the abstinences imposed by the Rule and by the Constitutions. Nevertheless, according to the traditional teaching of canonists, all Superiors in a clerical exempt religious Institute, unless they are expressly forbidden, may, in particular cases, dispense from the precepts of the Rule and the Constitutions which do not pertain to the very substance of the religious life.[81] In keeping with this principle, then, Capuchin Superiors may dispense their subjects in particular cases from the fasts and the abstinences imposed by the Rule and the Constitutions.

The traditional principle cited by canonists states that Superiors may dispense in *particular* cases. The Constitutions of the Friars Minor Conventual state that Superiors may dispense in *individual*

---

[78] *Constitutiones Generales Ordinis Fratrum Minorum, 1953,* art. 4, § 1, n. 2; art. 4, § 3.

[79] *Constitutiones Generales Ordinis Fratrum Minorum, 1953,* art. 4, § 1, n. 3; art. 3.

[80] *Constitutiones Ordinis Fratrum Minorum Sancti Patris Francisci Conventualium, 1932,* n. 322.

[81] Schaefer, *De Religiosis* (4. ed., Romae: Typis Polyglottis Vaticanis, 1947), n. 464; Michiels, *Normae Generales Juris Canonici,* II, 722–726; Van Hove, *De Privilegiis, De Dispensationibus* (Romae: Dessain, 1939), n. 423; Vermeersch-Creusen, *Epitome Iuris Canonici,* I, n. 193; Victorius ab Appeltern, *Compendium Praelectionum Juris Regularis* (editio altera, Parisiis, 1913), p. 383; Piatus Montensis, *Praelectiones Juris Regularis,* I, 572–573; Ledwolorz, "De Superiorum potestate dispensandi in iure particulari Ordinis Fratrum Minorum," *Antonianum,* XIII (1938), 42–46; Rodericus, *Quaestiones Regulares et Canonicae,* I, 172; Bernardino da Siena, *Esposizione della Regola Francescana,* n. 715; Albertus a Bulsano, *Expositio Regulae FF. Minorum, 1932,* n. 506.

cases.[82] In both these instances, it seems reasonable to affirm that the meaning of the words *particular* and *individual* may sometimes be extended beyond those cases which apply exclusively to individual physical subjects. The faculty granted is not to dispense particular or individual *Friars,* but to dispense in particular or in individual *cases.*

When any Superior grants a dispensation in favor of all the Friars who are subject to him, that dispensation is a *general* dispensation. In virtue of their ordinary powers, Franciscan Superiors cannot grant such a dispensation from the Rule and from the Constitutions of the Order. When a Superior, however, grants a dispensation in favor only of certain groups of his subjects or in favor of certain individual subjects, that dispensation is not a *general* dispensation. It is a dispensation granted in a *particular* or an *individual* case. Among the Friars Minor Conventual, therefore, and among the Friars Minor Capuchin, a local Superior can never dispense his entire community as such. He can dispense only individual members of that community. A Minister Provincial cannot dispense an entire province. He can, however, dispense individual friaries as well as individual Friars. The Minister General, finally, can dispense individual provinces, individual friaries, and individual Friars.[83]

Furthermore, parallel to the power which they possess of dispensing from the obligation of the fasts imposed by the common law when the cause for the dispensation is verified in every subject, Franciscan Superiors may dispense entire groups, no matter how large, or entire communities, by way of a single act, from the obligation of a fast or of an abstinence which has been imposed by the law of the Order.

Section 3. Dispensations from the Rule and the Constitutions According to the Special Faculties of Superiors

The difficulties contingent on the second World War were the

---

[82] *Constitutiones Ordinis Fratrum Minorum Sancti Patris Francisci Conventualium, 1932,* n. 322: "A lege ieiunii et abstinentiae . . . in casibus singularibus . . . Superiores . . . dispensare possunt suos subditos."

[83] Cf. Trienekens, *Expositio Canonico-Moralis Regulae Fratrum Minorum,* n. 126.

occasion for a notable change in the discipline of fast and abstinence also in the Franciscan Order. The generous dispensations which the Holy See granted to the faithful in general had their counterpart among the Franciscans. Each branch of the Order, however, met the situation in a somewhat different way. For that reason, the special discipline in force in the Order since 1941 will be considered separately in relation to the various branches.

1. THE ORDER OF FRIARS MINOR

The Procurator General of the Order of Friars Minor found occasion to ask for a specific concession with regard to the fasts imposed by the Franciscan Rule when the Sacred Congregation of the Council, on December 20, 1940, promulgated an indult concerning fast and abstinence for the dioceses of Italy for the year 1941.[84] The Procurator General's petition and the reply which he received are as follows:

> Most Blessed Father,
>
> Constrained by needs which each day grow worse in consequence of the contingencies of the war, the Procurator General of the Order of Friars Minor, with the consent of the Minister General, for the tranquillity of consciences, humbly implores the following indults, to be valid for as long as the present conditions endure:
>
> 1) That in Italy our religious may validly use, even on the days when the law of fast binds merely from the Rule, the indult of the Sacred Congregation of the Council,

[84] "Si rende noto che, attese le speciali circostanze del momento, la Santità di Nostro Signore Pio Pp. XII f. r. si è benignamente degnata di dispensare in Italia dalla legge del digiuno e dell'astinenza per l'anno 1941, ferma restando tale legge per il Mercoledì delle Ceneri e il Venerdì Santo.

Si esortano però vivamente i fedeli tutti, e in modo speciale il clero secolare, i religiosi e le religiose, a compensare in qualche modo con volontari esercizi di cristiana mortificazione ed espiazione, con il moltiplicare le opere di bene, soprattutto della carità verso i sofferenti e i bisognosi, ed unendosi con la preghiera alle sante intenzioni del Sommo Pontefice.

Roma, 20 dicembre 1940.

F. Card. Marmaggi, *Prefetto.*

G. Bruno, *Segretario.*"—

AAS, XXXIII (1941), 24; *AOFM,* LX (1941), 48.

given on December 20, 1940, and also eventual prorogations of this indult.

2) That our religious outside Italy, even on days on which the law of fast obliges only from the Rule, may use indults which are granted by local ordinaries in the name of the Holy See in places where they are burdened with economic hardships because of the war.

And may God etc.

In virtue of the faculties granted by our Most Holy Lord, and attentive to the petitions presented, the Sacred Congregation in Charge of the Affairs of Religious Institutes benignly authorized the Most Reverend Father Minister General, according to his prudent judgment and according to his conscience, to grant the favor stated in the petitions for as long as the present conditions endure.

All things to the contrary notwithstanding.

Given at Rome, March 3, 1941.

Vincent Cardinal La Puma, *Prefect.*

✠Fr. L. H. Pasetto, *Secretary.*[85]

Inasmuch as the benefits of the indult were granted not directly to the Friars of the Order, but only indirectly and through the agency of the Minister General, its practical application was

---

85 "Beatissime Pater,

Necessitatibus victus quotidiani ingravescentibus propter bellicos eventus, humilis Procurator Generalis O. F. M., de consensu sui Ministri Generalis, pro conscientiarum tranquillitate sequentia humiliter implorat indulta, perdurantibus praesentibus rerum adiunctis valitura:

1) Ut in Italia nostri Religiosi uti valeant, etiam diebus quibus ex Regula tantum viget lex ieiunii, Indulto a S. Congregatione Concilii, die 20 decembris anni 1940, concesso, eiusque eventualibus prorogationibus.

2) Ut extra Italiam nostri Religiosi, etiam diebus quibus ex Regula tantum viget lex ieiunii, uti possint Indultis, quae ab Ordinariis locorum, nomine S. Sedis, conceduntur in locis, quae ob bellum angustiis oeconomicis premuntur.

Et Deus, etc.

Vigore facultatum a Ss.mo Domino Nostro concessarum, S. Congregatio Negotiis Religiosorum Sodalium praeposita, attentis expositis, Rev.mo P. Ministro Generali benigne commisit, ut, pro suo arbitrio et conscientia, gratiam iuxta preces concedat perdurantibus praesentibus rerum adiunctis.

Contrariis quibuscumque non obstantibus.

Datum Romae, die 3 Martii 1941.

Vinc. Card. La Puma, *Praef.*

✠Fr. L. H. Pasetto, *Secret.*"—
AOFM, LX (1941), 72.

suspended until the Minister General had promulgated it. This he did on March 7, 1941, with certain added conditions:

> In virtue of the above apostolic rescript, we concede the favor requested according to the petition for as long as the present situation exists, and according to our mind.
>
> Rome, March 7, 1941.
>
> Fr. Leonard M. Bello, Minister General, O.F.M.
>
> Our mind is this:
>
> Ministers Provincial, in communicating to their subjects the above noted concession according to the spirit and the letter of the indult of the Sacred Congregation of the Council of December of the past year, are to take care:
>
> 1) That all our religious, wherever they be in the service of the Lord, shall strive to make compensation for the granted concessions by way of voluntary acts of mortification and penance, among which these are particularly recommended: a) a visit to the Blessed Sacrament made in common after dinner or after supper; b) the chanting or the reciting of the Litany of the Saints at night prayers; c) the salutary exercise of discipline and of the Way of the Cross performed for the aforesaid purpose.
>
> 2) that, whether they perform acts of mortification and of piety in particular or in common, our religious do so in union with the intentions of the Supreme Pontiff, Pope Pius XII, whom may God long keep in good health.[86]

[86] "Superioris Apostolici Rescripti vigore concedimus petitam gratiam iuxta preces, perdurantibus praesentibus rerum adiunctis, et ad mentem.

Romae, die 7 Martii 1941.

Fr. Leonardus M. Bello, *Min. G.lis O. F. M.*

Mens nostra haec est:

Ministri Provinciales communicantes suis subditis supra relatam concessionem, iuxta spiritum et litteram Indulti S. C. Concilii diei 20 Decembris superioris anni curent:

1) ut omnes religiosi nostri ubique terrarum Domino famulantes, factas sibi concessiones compensare satagant voluntariis mortificationis et pietatis exercitiis, inter quae haec praecipue Superioribus commendantur: a) Statio Ss. Sacramenti in communi, post prandium vel coenam facienda; b) Litaniae Sanctorum in functione vespertina cantandae vel recitandae; c) Salutare disciplinae, necnon pium Viae Crucis exercitium, in praefatum finem item peragendum;

2) ut sive in particularibus, sive in communibus mortificationis et pietatis actibus sese exerceant, Religiosi nostri sanctis intentionibus Summi Pontificis

It can be seen that the terms of this indult are not exactly the same as those set forth in the rescript of the Holy See to Cardinal Segura. That rescript implied that religious were automatically included in the dispensations granted by local ordinaries in virtue of the special faculties received by them on December 19, 1941. The indult given to the Order of Friars Minor seems to make such inclusion dependent upon a further concession of the Holy See. The discrepancy, however, is more apparent than real.

The interpretation issued to Cardinal Segura looked to the faculties issued to the bishops of the world on December 19, 1941. These faculties were not yet in existence at the time when the indult was granted to the Order of Friars Minor. The indult, on the other hand, was directly concerned only with the faculties which had been granted to the Bishops of Italy on December 20, 1940. Indirectly, of course, the indult had reference to future faculties of a like nature, but not in such a way as to predetermine the scope of those future concessions. The indult would have to be interpreted in the light of the faculties that would be granted in the future, and not the faculties in the light of the indult.

As will be seen from an interpretation which was later published in the *Acta Ordinis Fratrum Minorum,* the indult, at least for the future, did nothing more than grant the Friars an explicit permission to use the dispensations granted by local ordinaries from the fasts prescribed by the Rule. Of itself, it contained no direct dispensation. It had the further effect of settling any doubt with regard to the extension of the faculties of local ordinaries to the special fasts imposed by the Rule in the Order of Friars Minor.

After the Sacred Congregation of the Council, in the year 1949, had expressed its decision to restore the common law of fast and abstinence, at least in part,[87] the Minister General of the Order of Friars Minor, the Most Reverend Pacificus Perantoni, published the following ordinance:

> We decree that the observance of fasting prescribed by our Holy Mother the Church and by our Holy Rule be

Pii PP. XII, quem Deusdiu incolumen servet, suas sociare contendant."—*AOFM,* LX (1941), 72–73.

[87] *AAS,* XLI (1949), p. 32.

restored to its pristine vigor in the whole Order of Friars Minor.

The serious problems confronting the world, the dangers threatening Holy Church in many nations, the ever increasing and spreading relaxation of morals, and many other kinds of evils; furthermore the necessity of calling on the divine assistance for an ever greater increase in our Order; all these things are just so many motives which should urge every religious to foster, not only a fervent religious spirit, but also a spirit of mortification and penance; we earnestly exhort, therefore, each and everyone of our Sons in Saint Francis willingly to accept this salutary disposition with a truly supernatural spirit, and thus efficaciously to promote the glory of God in the world and the increase of our Order.

Given at Rome from our General Curia, November 21, 1950.

Fr. Pacificus Perantoni
Minister General O.F.M.[88]

As can be seen from this ordinance of the Minister General, the concessions granted to the Friars of his Order through their Ministers Provincial under date of March 7, 1941, are not revoked. The General expressed his mind that the discipline of the Rule and of the Church should be restored, but he did not enforce such a restoration through a withdrawal of the past concessions.

---

[88] "Statuimus ut in toto Ordine Fratrum Minorum observantia ieiunii, a sancta Matre Ecclesia et a sancta nostra Regula praescripta, in pristinum vigorem restituatur.

Gravia problemata mundum agitantia, pericula in multis nationibus sanctam Ecclesiam minitantia, semper crescens et maiorem extensionem assumens relaxatio morum, atque plurimae aliae species mali; insuper necessitas invocandi divinum auxilium ad semper maius incrementum Ordinis nostri; haec omnia totidem motiva sunt, quae omnem Religiosum incitare debent ad colendum, praeter fervidam religiositatem, etiam spiritum mortificationis et poenitentiae; omnes igitur et singulos Filios in S. Francisco enixe exhortamur, ut hanc salutarem dispositionem cum vero spiritu supernaturali accipere velint, atque ita efficaciter promovere gloriam Dei in mundo et incrementum Ordinis nostri.

Datum Romae, e nostra Curia generali, die 21 Novembris, 1950.

Fr. Pacificus Perantoni
Min. Gen. O.F.M."—

AOFM, LXIX (1951), p. 291, n. 3, 1.

This is confirmed by a very interesting and a most enlightening subsequent doctrinal interpretation of the discipline of the fast in the Order of Friars Minor. Although the interpretation possesses no official character, it is of great authority, first of all because it is found in the official publication of the Order, the *Acta Ordinis Fratrum Minorum,* and secondly because of the unquestionably high authority of its authors, all of them outstanding Franciscan canonists. The interpretation follows:

> 1. Whether a dispensation from the law of fast and abstinence given by local ordinaries in virtue of the indult granted by the Sacred Congregation of the Council on January 28, 1949, is valid also for the fasts imposed by the Rule of the Friars Minor:
>
> a) if there is express mention made of regulars in the dispensation.
>
> *Answer.* Attentive to the mind of the Sacred Congregation of the Council, in the Affirmative.
>
> b) if it is given generally for the territory, without any express mention.
>
> *Answer.* In the Affirmative (at least probably).
>
> c) if it is expressly given only from the common law.
>
> *Answer.* In the Negative.
>
> And if in the negative:
>
> 2. Whether a dispensation given as above under number 1 has force for the fasts of the Friars Minor by reason of the rescript of the Sacred Congregation of Religious of March 3, 1941.
>
> *Answer.* In the Affirmative.
>
> And if in the affirmative:
>
> 3. Can Ministers Provincial of the Order of Friars Minor together with their Definitories impose the obligation of the fast regardless of whether it derives from the Rule or from the common law?
>
> *Answer.* They cannot urge the obligation (since it has already been legitimately suppressed), but they can impose it by a special precept, whose degree of obligation will depend upon the intention of these Superiors.
>
> 4. What force is to be attributed to the ordinance of the Minister General of the Order of Friars Minor of November 21, 1950?
>
> *Answer.* Provision for this is made in the answer to the third question.

Rome, the Pontifical Athenaeum Antonianum, October 20, 1951.

Father Cosmas Sartori
Father Adolph Ledwolorz
Father Guy Brisebois [89]

Although this interpretation is given specifically with a view to the discipline of the fast in the Order of Friars Minor according to the terms of the indult granted to that branch of the Franciscan Order on March 3, 1941, the principles which it presents have a much wider application. Under number 1. above, the responses given attribute to local ordinaries the faculty to dispense or not to dispense from the fasts of the Franciscan Rule, as they will. This can have but one meaning, namely that the power to dispense or not to dispense from these fasts rests in the hands of local ordi-

---

[89] "1. Utrum dispensatio a lege ieiunii et abstinentiae data ab Ordinariis locorum vi indulti, a S. Congregatione Concilii concessi die 28 Ianuarii 1949, valeat etiam pro ieiuniis Regulae Fratrum Minorum; et quidem

a) si in dispensatione expressa mentio fiat Regularium.

Resp. Attenta mente S. Congregationis Concilii, affirmative.

b) si detur generaliter pro territorio, sine ulla expressa mentione.

Resp. Affirmative (saltem probabiliter).

c) si detur expresse solum a lege communi.

Resp. Negative.

Et si negative:

2. Utrum dispensatio data ut supra sub n. 1 valeat pro ieiuniis Regulae Fratrum Minorum vi rescripti S. Congregationis de Religiosis diei 3 Martii 1941.

Resp. Affirmative.

Et si affirmative:

3. Possuntne Ministri Provinciales O.F.M. cum suo Definitorio imponere obligationem ieiunii sive Regulae sive legis communis?

Resp. Non possunt urgere obligationem (utpote iam legitime suppressam), sed possunt id imponere per speciale praeceptum, cuius obligationis gradus pendet ab horum Superiorum intentione.

4. Quaenam vis tribuenda est ordinationi Ministri Generalis O.F.M. die 21 Nov. 1950?

Resp. Provisum in responsione ad tertium.

Romae, ex Pontificio Athenaeo Antoniano, die 20 Octobris 1951.

P. Cosmas Sartori

P. Adulphus Ledwolorz

P. Guidus Brisebois."—

AOFM, LXX (1951), 423.

naries, not by reason of this indult of March 3, 1941, but by reason of the special faculties which the ordinaries themselves possess. The indult, therefore, does not contain a dispensation of any kind. Rather, it contains simply an explicit permission by reason of which the Friars may licitly use dispensations from local ordinaries with regard to the fasts imposed by the Rule.

The principles enumerated in that same number confirm what was said previously about the applicability of the dispensations of local ordinaries to the fasts imposed by the Rule. The authors of the interpretation find no difficulty in determining the effect of the dispensations of local ordinaries upon the obligation of the fasts prescribed in the Rule when these ordinaries make their intention manifest, as in numbers 1. a) and 1. b) above. They do not have that same certainty, however, when local ordinaries grant a dispensation from the fast without making mention of religious. Nevertheless, even in this case they teach that the Franciscans are at least probably dispensed from the obligation of the fasts ordered by the Rule. In such cases the local ordinary is presumed to have used his special faculties to their fullest extent and to have dispensed the Franciscans even from the special fasts imposed by their own law.

Principle number 3. above is of the greatest importance for practical questions of conscience. It declares that, although a local ordinary has granted a dispensation, Ministers Provincial with their Definitories can, by way of a special precept, impose fasts as they are enjoined by the common law or by the Rule, but cannot urge these obligations as if they bound from the common law or from the Rule. The reason is evident. Once a local ordinary has granted a dispensation from the fast according to the full extent of his special faculties, that dispensation automatically removes the obligations imposed by the common law and by the Rule. The Minister Provincial and his Definitory cannot urge an obligation that no longer exists. Therefore, if they choose to impose these fasts by special precept, the fasts will bind only by reason of the precept, and not by reason of the common law or of the Rule, and they will bind only in the manner and to the extent that these Superiors intend for them.

2. THE ORDER OF FRIARS MINOR CAPUCHIN

Shortly after the Procurator General of the Order of Friars Minor had requested and received a special indult for his branch of the Order from the Sacred Congregation of Religious, the Procurator General of the Capuchins made a similar request. The petition and the reply of the Sacred Congregation of Religious, under date of December 20, 1941, follow:

> Most Blessed Father,
>
> Attentive to the present sufferings and hardships of the war, Father Leonard of Forosarsinio, Procurator General of the Order of Friars Minor Capuchin, prostrate at the feet of Your Holiness, humbly implores an Apostolic Indult in virtue of which the individual Major Superiors of the Order may have the faculty of dispensing their own subjects from the precepts of fast and abstinence imposed by the Rule or by the Constitutions according to the terms of the dispensations from fasts and abstinences imposed by ecclesiastical law on all the faithful which the Apostolic See, or local ordinaries, and other ecclesiastical authorities have granted or will grant in different places for as long as these same circumstances last.
>
> And may God etc. . . .
>
> In virtue of the faculties granted by Our Most Holy Lord, the Sacred Congregation in Charge of the Affairs of Religious Institutes, attentive to the petition, has benignly committed to the Most Reverend Father Minister General the power to concede the favor requested according to his prudent judgment and conscience for as long as present conditions last.
>
> All things to the contrary notwithstanding.
>
> Given at Rome, December 20, 1941.
>
> Vincent Cardinal La Puma, *Prefect.*
>
> ✠Fr. L. H. Pasetto, *Secretary.*[90]

---

[90] "Beatissime Pater,

Fr. Leonardus a Forosarsinio, Procurator Generalis Ordinis Fratrum Minorum Capuccinorum, attentis praesentibus belli discriminibus et angustiis, ad pedes S. V. provolutus, humiliter implorat apostolicum indultum vi cuius singulis Ordinis Superioribus Maioribus facultas competat proprios subditos dispensandi super praeceptis ieiunii et abstinentiae a Regula vel Constitutionibus impositis, iuxta terminos dispensationum quas Sedes Apostolica vel Ordinarii locorum aliaeque ecclesiasticae auctoritates, pro diversitate locorum,

Three days after the granting of the indult, the Capuchin Minister General, Father Donatus of Welle, made it operative by the following decree of execution:

> In virtue of the faculties benignly granted to Us by the foregoing Apostolic Rescript, we concede the favor requested to the aforesaid Major Superiors of our Order, namely: to the Ministers and Commissaries Provincial; to the Commissaries General; to the Superiors Regular of Missions; and to Custodes Provincial according to the clauses and the conditions of the same Rescript. Let them with all caution not use the faculty for dispensing, except in true necessity and with the assignment to their respective subjects of some exercise of penance or of piety, with the due observance of all things required by law.
>
> Rome, from our General Curia, December 23, 1941.
>
> Father Donatus of Welle,
> *Minister General O.F.M.Cap.*[91]

---

iisdem adiunctis perdurantibus, concesserunt vel concedent in favorem fidelium quoad ieiunia et abstinentias a lege ecclesiastica omnibus fidelibus imposita.

Et Deus etc. . . .

Vigore facultatum a SS.mo Domino Nostro concessarum, Sacra Congregatio Negotiis Religiosorum Sodalium praeposita, attentis expositis, Rev.mo P. Ministro Generali benigne commisit ut petitam gratiam iuxta preces pro suo arbitrio et conscientia concedat, perdurantibus praesentibus rerum adiunctis.

Contrariis quibuscumque non obstantibus.

Datum Romae, die 20 decembris 1941.

Vinc. Card. La Puma, *Praefectus.*

✠Fr. L. H. Pasetto, *Secretarius.*"—

AOFMC, LVII (1941), 184.

[91] "Vigore facultatum per antecedens Apostolicum Rescriptum Nobis benigne tributarum, enunciatis Superioribus Maioribus Ordinis Nostri, scilicet, Ministris et Commissariis Provincialibus, Commissariis Generalibus, Superioribus Regularibus Missionum atque Custodibus Provincialibus petitam gratiam concedimus sub clausulis et conditionibus eiusdem Rescripti, cauto ne facultate dispensandi utantur nisi in vera necessitate et imposito suis cuiusque subditis alio poenitentiae vel pietatis exercitio, servatisque de iure servandis.

Romae, ex Curia Nostra Generali, die 23 decembris 1941.

Fr. Donatus a Welle, *Min. Gen. O.F.M.Cap.*"—

AOFMC, LVII (1941), 184.

On the same day Father Donatus issued a general directive concerning the Friars' use of dispensations when granted either by local ordinaries or by major Superiors in virtue of the special faculties possessed by them:

> In virtue of the preceding documents, namely: of the Communication of the Sacred Congregation for Extraordinary Ecclesiastical Affairs (of December 19, 1941) and of the Rescript of the Sacred Congregation of Religious, all of our Religious, for as long as the present circumstances endure, may, with a safe conscience, use dispensations which legitimate ecclesiastical Authority, or their respective Major Superiors of the Order, have conceded or will concede, both with regard to fast and abstinence as prescribed by the Church, and also with regard to fast and abstinence as imposed by the Rule and by the Constitutions of our Order, observing, moreover, the ordinances and the exhortations which have been stated in these same documents.
>
> Given at Rome, from our General Curia, December 23, 1941.
>
> Father Donatus of Welle,
> *Minister General O.F.M.Cap.*[92]

The special faculties for dispensing from the fasts and the abstinences imposed by the Rule and the Constitutions which were granted to the major Superiors of the Capuchin Order have no direct connection with the faculties possessed by local ordinaries. Nevertheless, they were granted according to the same terms as these latter faculties. Capuchin major Superiors have the same power to dispense from the fasts and the abstinences prescribed

[92] "Virtute praecedentium documentorum, *Communicationis* scilicet S. Congregationis pro Negotiis Ecclesiasticis Extraordinariis, necnon *Rescripti* S. Congregationis de Religiosis, omnes nostri Religiosi, perdurantibus praesentibus adiunctis, tum quoad ieiunium et abstinentiam ab Ecclesia praescripta, tum quoad illa a Regula et Constitutionibus Ordinis nostri imposita, tuta conscientia uti possunt dispensationibus quas legitima Auctoritas ecclesiastica, vel respective Superiores Maiores Ordinis concesserunt aut concedent, servatis tamen ordinationibus et exhortationibus ab Ipsis statutis vel statuendis.

Datum Romae, e Curia Nostra Generali, die 23 dec. 1941.

Fr. Donatus a Welle, *Min. Gen. O.F.M.Cap.*"—
AOFMC, LVII (1941), 184.

by the Rule and the Constitutions which local ordinaries have for dispensing from fast and abstinence in general. From this it can be seen that Capuchin major Superiors may dispense their subjects even in a general way from the obligation of the fasts and abstinences imposed by the Rule and the Constitutions, and that they may use these faculties under the same conditions that are required for local ordinaries to use the special faculties which they possess. According to the decree of execution of the Minister General, when they grant such dispensations, these major Superiors should impose some exercise of piety or of penance upon their subjects.

Capuchin major Superiors are completely independent of local ordinaries in their use of these faculties. If the requisite conditions are verified, a Capuchin Superior may dispense from the law of the Order even when the local ordinary does not dispense from the law of the Church. Usually it will not be advisable for them to use their faculties in this manner. Yet, according to their strict right, should the need arise, they have the power to do so.

The mere fact that their major Superiors have the power of dispensing from the fasts and the abstinences prescribed by the Rule and the Constitutions in no way deprives Capuchins who are subjects of any benefits which they might be able to obtain with regard to these obligations through the dispensations of local ordinaries. Their Superiors can forbid them to make use of such dispensations. But in such a case, since the original obligation has been removed by means of the dispensation, the Friars will be bound to observe these fasts and abstinences, not as imposed by the Rule or by the Constitutions, but as imposed through a precept of their Superiors.

When, on January 28, 1949, the Holy See issued to local ordinaries a somewhat modified renewal of their special faculties, the Minister General of the Friars Minor Capuchin took this occasion to publish the following directive concerning the manner in which the major Superiors of the Order should use their particular special faculties:

> Since by a Decree of the Sacred Congregation of the Council it has recently been declared that the law of abstinence and fast which had previously been somewhat relaxed because of adverse circumstances should be re-

stored, at least in part, with the coming of the propitious time of the Holy Year, by this very fact, namely, inasmuch as the conditions which were formerly verified are no longer considered to endure, the concessions and the declarations made by our Predecessor in virtue of apostolic faculties cease.

Since, however, the restoration of the aforesaid law pertains to the common discipline, it is clear that our Friars may licitly conform to the prescriptions of the Church with regard to fast and abstinence.

Since conditions have changed, however, the fasts and the abstinences which are imposed in virtue of the Rule and the Constitutions, and whose relaxation had been committed to the Superiors of Provinces, Commissariates, Missions, and Custodies, are to be restored in their entirety, unless it appears to these Superiors that some other arrangement should be made in particular cases and circumstances of either a personal or a local character.

In the manner, however, in which the Holy See wished them to be advised, our religious should be mindful that in these most serious times it is proper for religious not to be remiss, but rather to increase in their practice of voluntary Christian perfection and in the works of charity, whenever it is permitted to Superiors to temper the rigor of the fast and the abstinence.

Rome, February 10, 1949.

Father Clement of Milwaukee,
Minister General, O.F.M.Cap.[93]

[93] "Cum per Decretum S. Congregationis Concilii nuper declaratum fuerit legem abstinentiae et ieiunii, ob adversa rerum adiuncta antea quadamtenus relaxatam, saltem ex parte, adveniente propitio Anni Sancti tempore, restaurandam esse, hoc ipso decidunt concessiones et declarationes a Praedecessore Nostro, vigore facultatum apostolicarum, factae, quatenus nempe iam perdurare haud censentur adiuncta tunc vigentia.

Quia vero restauratio praefatae legis, communem respicit disciplinam, clarum est Fratribus nostris licere eidem sese conformare quoad ieiunia et abstinentiam ab Ecclesia praescripta.

Ieiunia autem et abstinentiae quae vi Regulae et Constitutionum Ordinis imponuntur, quorum relaxatio commissa fuerat Superioribus Provinciarum, Commissariatuum, Missionum et Custodiarum, evolutis rerum adiunctis, restauranda penitus sunt, nisi aliud decernere ipsis videatur in casibus et adiunctis pecularibus sive personarum sive locorum.

Omnes autem sodales nostri meminerint proprium esse religiosorum, prouti ipsos monitos voluit S. Sedis, 'gravissimis hisce temporibus voluntaria

The foregoing notice of the Minister General does not, of itself, deprive major Superiors of their special faculties. It directs how these faculties are to be used; and it declares that, when the reasons which prompted the granting of these special concessions have ceased, by that very fact the concessions themselves have come to cease. The will of the Minister General is this: major Superiors should restore the perfect observance of the fasts and the abstinences prescribed by the Rule and the Constitutions within the limits of their respective jurisdictions, unless special circumstances demand their continued relaxation.

Although Father Clement's directive does not mention dispensations from the fasts and the abstinences imposed by the Rule and the Constitutions which might have been given by local ordinaries, there is no doubt that he wished the Friars to abstain from the use of these dispensations. It was his stated will that the observance of the fasts and the abstinences imposed by the Rule and the Constitutions should be restored in their entirety. This could hardly be effected if the Friars continued to make use of dispensations from such fasts and abstinences when granted by local ordinaries.

3. THE ORDER OF FRIARS MINOR CONVENTUAL

Unlike the Order of Friars Minor and the Order of Friars Minor Capuchin, the Order of Friars Minor Conventual received no special indults dealing with fast and abstinence during this past war. A response of the Sacred Congregation of Religious, however, of January 28, 1941, and a communication of the Minister General on January 30 of that year declared that the particular law of the Order on fast and abstinence did not cease for the friars in Italy by reason of the dispensations published by the Holy Father for that country for the year 1941.[94]

christianae perfectionis exercitia nec non caritatis opera' haud remittere, sed potius augere, quotiescumque vigor ieiunii et abstinentiae a Superioribus temperari permittatur.

Romae, 10 februarii 1949.

Fr. Clemens a Milwaukee, *Min. Gen. O.F.M.Cap.*"—*AOFMC*, LXV (1949), 20.

[94] *COFMC*, XXXVIII (1941), 47.

Later that same year, a communication was issued by the Secretariate General of the Order with the intention of providing the Friars with a practical norm to follow regarding the effect which dispensations of local ordinaries in general had upon the obligation of the fasts and the abstinences imposed by the law of the Order. The communication used two sources for establishing this norm.

The first of these sources was a declaration of the Holy Office, dated April 21, 1907, which received papal confirmation on May 1 of the same year. This declaration stated that the particular obligations of religious were not comprehended in the special regulations on fast and abstinence which had been published in Italy for the year 1907.[95] The second norm is canon 620.[96]

No explanation of the declaration or of the canon is offered. They are presented simply as authentic norms from the past, and therefore as safe rules for the Friars to follow in the future when local ordinaries come to grant dispensations from fast and abstinence during the war. In such cases, according to the norms presented, the Friars could not take advantage of these dispensations with regard to the fasts and the abstinences prescribed by the Rule and the Constitutions.

These norms, however, were not imposed as of obligation. They were suggested as a safe course of action. Hence, when it became clear that the Franciscans too could benefit from dispensations granted by local ordinaries in virtue of their faculties, even for fasts and abstinences prescribed in their special law, the Conventual Friars also could make valid use of such dispensations. For the rest, the Friars had to rely on the power for dispensing which their Superiors possessed in virtue of their ordinary faculties.

An unpublished letter of the Minister General of the Friars Minor Conventual, dated December 5, 1955, expresses his present mind regarding the observance of fast and abstinence by the Friars of his branch of the Order:

> We ask our Friars regularly to observe the fasts and

[95] *ASS,* XL (1907), 469.

[96] *COFMC,* XXXVIII (1941), 87-88.

> abstinences which before the World War were also observed in the universal Church. Nevertheless, when there is present a sufficient reason, Superiors can freely dispense their subjects.[97]

Thus, in conformity with the will of the other two Ministers General, it is the will of the Minister General of the Friars Minor Conventual to restore, in his branch of the Order, the full observance of all the fasts and abstinences, inclusive of all that are prescribed in the general Church law. Only in a case of true necessity are Superiors to dispense from these obligations.

---

[97] "Fratres nostros rogamus ut ieiunia et abstinentias regulariter servent quae etiam in universali Ecclesia ante mundiale bellum servabantur. Quando vero ratio sufficiens adest, Superiores possunt libere suos subditos dispensare." —From the archives of Saint Bonaventure's Friary, Washington, D. C.

CONCLUSIONS

1. There is a special equivalent precept of the Franciscan Rule to observe the "Lent" which begins on the Feast of All Saints and lasts until Christmas, and to observe every Friday as a day of fast.

2. There is no special precept of the Franciscan Rule to observe the Lent that precedes our Lord's Resurrection. The Rule simply calls to mind the precept established in the common law.

3. With the advent of the law of the Code there is no obligation for Franciscans to fast when Christmas falls on a Friday, and, unless it has been imposed from some other source, there is no obligation for the Friars to fast or to abstain when any holy day of obligation falls on a day of fast or of abstinence prescribed by the law of the Order.

4. Even though the "Lent of Benediction" is not of obligation, the Franciscans are obliged to fast on the Fridays which occur during that Lent.

5. Only those Franciscans who fall between the ages of twenty-one and fifty-nine are obliged to observe the fasts prescribed in the Rule, unless a more extensive obligation is imposed from some other source.

6. The same causes which excuse from the Church law on fasting suffice also to excuse the Franciscans from the fast prescribed by their Rule.

7. Since the Franciscan Rule presents simply a naked precept of fasting, the Franciscans, as long as they are otherwise not forbidden to do so, may in the fulfillment of their obligation make use of all the supplementary norms of the common law which concretely determine the nature of fasting.

8. Dispensations granted by local ordinaries in virtue of the power which they have from the Code avail for the Franciscans with regard to the fasts and the abstinences imposed by the common law, but not with regard to the fasts and the abstinences imposed by the special law of the Order.

9. Dispensations granted by local ordinaries in virtue of the special faculties which they received in 1941, 1946, and 1949 avail

for Franciscans with regard to the fasts and the abstinences prescribed by the common law, and probably even for those which are prescribed by the special law of the Order.

10. According to the power given to them by the Code, Franciscan Superiors can, in individual cases, dispense from the fasts and the abstinences prescribed by the common law.

11. According to the power which they have as Regular Superiors, Franciscan Superiors can, in particular cases, dispense from the fasts and the abstinences imposed in the Rule and the Constitutions.

12. In virtue of a special indult which the Order received in 1941, members of the Order of Friars Minor may validly and licitly make use of dispensations from fast granted by local ordinaries, even with regard to fasts of the Rule.

13. In virtue of an indult which the Order received in 1941, major Superiors of the Order of Friars Minor Capuchin may dispense from the fasts and the abstinences imposed by the Rule and the Constitutions according to the norm laid down in the indult granted to local ordinaries in 1941.

BIBLIOGRAPHY

SOURCES

General Sources

Acta Apostolicae Sedis, Commentarium Officiale, Romae, 1909—

Acta Sanctae Sedis, 41 vols., Romae, 1865–1908.

Codex Iuris Canonici Pii X Pontificis Maximi Iussu Digestus Benedicti Papae XV Auctoritate Promulgatus, Romae: Typis Polyglottis Vaticanis, 1917; Reimpressio, 1948.

Codicis Iuris Canonici Fontes, cura Em̃i Petri Card. Gasparri editi, 9 vols., Romae [later Civitate Vaticana]: Typis Polyglottis Vaticanis, 1923–1939. (Vols. VII–IX, ed. cura et studio Em̃i Iustiniani Card. Serédi.)

Corpus Iuris Canonici, 2 vols., Vol. II, Editio Lipsiensis Secunda, Richter-Friedberg, Lipsiae, 1881.

Magnum Bullarium Romanum, 18 vols., Luxemburgi, 1727–1754.

Sources Pertaining to the Franciscan Order

I. CONSTITUTIONS

1. Early Constitutions

"Constitutiones Generales Ordinis Fratrum Minorum Editae et Confirmatae in Capitulo Generali apud Narbonam A.D. 1260, Decima Iunii, Tempore Rev. P. Bonaventurae," *Archivum Franciscanum Historicum,* XXXIV (1941), 37–94; 284–337.—cited in the text as *Constitutiones Narbonenses.*

"Constitutiones Generales Editae in Capitulo Generali Assisiensi Anno 1279," *AFH,* XXXIV (1941), 37–94; 284–337.—cited in the text as *Constitutiones Assisienses, 1279.*

"Constitutiones Generales Editae in Capitulo Generali Parisiensi Anno 1292," *AFH,* XXXIV (1941), 37–94; 284–337.—cited in the text as *Constitutiones Parisienses, 1292.*

"Constitutiones Generales Ordinis Fratrum Minorum Anno 1316 Assisii Conditae," *AFH,* IV (1911), 269–302; 508–526.—cited in the text as *Constitutiones Assisienses, 1316.*

"Compilatio Lugdunensis ad Constitutiones Assisii, 1325," *AFH,* IV (1911), 526–536.

"Constitutiones Generales Magistri Geraldi de Equitania Ministri Generalis Ordinis Minorum Editae et Confirmatae in Capitulo Generali Celebrato apud Perpinianum Anno Domini, 1331," *AFH,* II (1909), 269–292; 412–430; 575–599.

"Ordinationes sive Statuta Benedicti XII, 28 Nov., 1336," *AFH,* XXX (1937), 309–390.

"Statuta Generalia Caturcensia, An. 1337," *AFH,* XXX (1937), 128–157.

"Constitutiones Capituli Generalis Assisii, 1340," AFH, VI (1913), 253–256. —cited in the text as *Constitutiones Assisienses, 1340.*

"Constitutiones Capituli Generalis Assisii Anno 1346, Venetiis," *AFH,* V (1912), 699–708.

"Statuta Generalia Lugdunensia, An. 1351," *AFH,* XXX (1937), 158–169.

"Constitutiones Generales Compilatae Assisii in Capitulo Ordinis Celebrato An. 1354," *AFH,* XXXV (1942), 35–112.—cited in the text as *Constitutiones Assisienses, 1354.*

"Constitutiones Martinianae, 1430," in Lucas Waddingus, *Annales Minorum,* 27 vols., Vol. X, 3. ed., curavit Josephus Maria Fonseca, Ad Claras Aquas, 1932, pp. 178–187.

"Constitutiones Julianae, 1508," *Franziskanische Studien,* IV (1916), 201–206.

2. Constitutions of the Friars Minor Conventual

"Statuta Sixtinae, 1469," *Miscellanea Franciscana,* XLV (1945), 94–132.

"Constitutiones Alexandrinae, 1500," in Dominicus De Gubernatis, *Orbis Seraphicus,* 6 vols., Vol. III, Romae, 1684, pp. 138–210.

"Constitutiones Pianae Ordinis Fratrum Minorum Conventualium, 17 Sept., 1565," in *Magnum Bullarium Romanum,* 18 vols., Vol. II, Luxemburgi, 1727, pp. 175–183.

Constitutiones Urbanae Ordinis Fratrum Minorum S. Francisci Conventualium, 1628, Assisi, 1803.—cited in the text as *Constitutiones Urbanae.*

Constitutiones Urbanae Fratrum Minorum S. Francisci Conventualium ad Breviorem Methodum Redactae Papa Clemente XIV, 1771, Romae, 1894.—cited in the text as *Constitutiones Urbano-Clementinae.*

Constitutiones Urbanae Ordinis Minorum S. P. Francisci Conventualium Auctoritate Pii VII. Pontificis Maximi Explanatae, 1823, Romae, 1823. —cited in the text as *Constitutiones Pio-Urbanae.*

Constitutiones Ordinis Fratrum Minorum Sancti Patris Francisci Conventualium, Romae: ad SS. XII Apostolos, 1932.

3. Constitutions of the Friars Minor of the Observant Families

"Constitutiones B. P. Ioannis de Capistrano super Regulam Fratrum Minorum sub Eugen. IV Anno 1443. Die 24 Sept. in Duodecim Capitula Distincte, & Observantibus Traditae," in Dominicus De Gubernatis, *Orbis Seraphicus,* III, pp. 95–105.

"Statuta Generalia Observantium Ultramontanorum An. 1451 Barcinonae Condita," *AFH*, XXXVIII (1945), 106–197.

Constitutiones Salmanticenses seu Monilianses, 1553, Romae, 1576.

"Constitutiones Vallisoletanae seu Calatayeronenses, 1593," in Dominicus De Gubernatis, *Orbis Seraphicus*, III, pp. 412–553.

"Constitutiones Reverendiss. Patris Bonaventurae Calatayeronensis Totius Ordinis Ministri Generalis pro Reformatis Fratribus in Provinciis Italiae Editae Romae Die 20. Iunii, 1595," in Dominicus De Gubernatis, *Orbis Seraphicus*, III, pp. 561–568.

"Statuta Generalia Barchinonensia Regularis Observantiae Seraphici Sancti Patris Nostri Francisci pro eius Cismontana Familia Novissime in Comitiis Generalibus Intermediis Segoviae Habitis Anno Domini 1621, sub Reverendo Patre Benigno a Genua, Totius Ordinis Generali Ministro Accuratius Revisa & Faciliori Methodo Disposita, Summo Patrum Consensu Recepta, & Approbata," in Dominicus De Gubernatis, *Orbis Seraphicus*, III, 621–704.

Statuti Generali delle Riforma de Minori Osservanti Cismontani, 1625, Roma, 1626.

Statuta, Constitutiones, et Decreta Generalia Familiae Cismontanae Ordinis S. Francisci de Observantia ex Omnibus Eiusdem Ordinis Constitutionibus et Statutis Collecta, & Restituta iuxta Sancitum in Capitulo Generali Romano Anni 1639, atque in Generali Congregatione Romana Anni 1642 Approbata, Romae, 1642.—cited in the text as *Constitutiones Romanae.*

"Le Constitutioni Generali per le Provincie Riformate Cismontane, 1642," in Dominicus De Gubernatis, *Orbis Seraphicus*, IV, pp. 87–113.

Constitutiones et Statuta Generalia Cismontanae Familiae Ordinis Sancti Francisci de Observantia ex Decretis Capitul. General. Romani Ann. 1639 & Toletani Ann. 1658 Compilata, et per S. Congregationem super Negotiis Episcoporum et Regularium Revisa, & Approbata, Reverendiss. P. Michaele Angelo de Sambuca, Romae, 1663.—cited in the text as *Constitutiones Sambucanae.*

Novissima pro Cismontana Minorum Familia Generalium Constitutionum Collectio Reverendissimi Patris F. Joannis a Capistrano, 1768, Romae, 1827.—cited in the text as *Constitutiones Capistranae.*

Statuta et Constitutiones Generales Familiae Cismontanae Ordinis S. Francisci Minorum Reformatorum, 1889, Ad Claras Aquas, 1890.

Constitutiones Generales Ordinis Minorum, 1889, Ad Claras Aquas, 1891.—cited in the text as *Constitutiones Aloysianae.*

Constitutiones Generales Fratrum Minorum, Romae, 1897.

Constitutiones Generales Fratrum Minorum, Ad Claras Aquas, 1914.

Constitutiones Generales Fratrum Minorum, Ad Claras Aquas, 1922.

Constitutiones Generales Ordinis Fratrum Minorum, Romae: Curiae Generalis Ordinis, 1953.

4. Constitutions of the Friars Minor Capuchin

"Costituzioni di Albacina, 1529," in *Le Prime Costituzioni dei Frati Minori Cappuccini,* Roma, 1913, pp. 17–31.

"Le Constitutione deli Frati Minori Detti Capuccini, 1536," in *Primigeniae Legislationis Ordinis Fratrum Minorum Capuccinorum Textus Originales,* Romae, 1928, pp. 356–419.

"Le Constitutioni de Frati Minori Detti Cappucini, 1552," in *Primigeniae Legislationis Ordinis Fratrum Minorum Capuccinorum Textus Originales,* pp. 356–419.

"Le Constitutioni de' Frati Minori Cappuccini, 1575," in *Le Prime Costituzioni dei Frati Minori Cappuccini,* pp. 35–100.

Constitutioni de' Frati Minori Cappuccini di San Francesco, 1575, Ferrara, 1577.

Constitutioni de Frati Minori Capucini, 1608, Roma, 1609.

Constitutions Reguliers des Frères Mineurs Capucins de l'Ordre d Sainct Francois, 1608, Lyon, 1623.

Constitutiones Fratrum Minorum Sancti Francisci Capuccinorum, 1638, Romae, 1638.

Constitutioni dei Frati Minori Cappuccini, 1638, Roma, 1638.

Le Constituzioni dei Frati Minori Cappuccini, 1643, Palermo, 1854.

Constitutions of the Friars Minor Capuchin of Saint Francis, 1643, Newport, 1875.

Constitutiones Fratrum Minorum S. Francisci Capuccinorum, 1909, Romae, 1909.

Constitutiones Fratrum Minorum Capuccinorum, 1925, editio altera, Romae, 1931.

Rule and Testament of the Seraphic Father Saint Francis and Constitutions of the Capuchin Friars Minor of Saint Francis, 1925, Detroit: Province of Saint Joseph of the Capuchin Order, 1945.

II. Other Franciscan Sources

Acta Ordinis Fratrum Minorum, Romae, 1882—

Analecta Ordinis Fratrum Minorum Capuccinorum, Romae, 1885—

Bullarium Franciscanum, Vol. I–IV, Romae, 1759–1768; Vols. V–VII, Romae, 1898–1904; Series nova, Vols. I–III, Ad Claras Aquas, 1929–1949.

Bullarium Ordinis FF. Minorum S. P. Francisci Capuccinorum, Vols. I–VII, Romae, 1740–1752; Vols. VII–X, Oeniponte, 1883–1884.—cited in the text as *Bullarium Capuccinorum.*

Caeremoniale Romano-Seraphicum ad Usum Ordinis Fratrum Minorum Capuccinorum, Romae: Apud Curiam Generalem O.F.M.Cap., 1944.

Commentarium Ordinis Fratrum Minorum Conventualium, Romae, 1904—

Le Prime Costituzioni dei Frati Minori Cappuccini, Roma, 1913.

Monumenta ad Constitutiones Ordinis Fratrum Minorum Capuccinorum Pertinentia, Romae, 1916.

Ordinationes et Decisiones Capitulorum Generalium Ordinis Fratrum Minorum Sancti Francisci Capuccinorum, Romae, 1851.

Ordinationes Capitulorum Generalium Ordinis Minorum Capuccinorum, Romae, 1928.

Primigeniae Legislationis Ordinis Fratrum Minorum Capuccinorum Textus Originales, ed. Eduardus Alenconiensis, Romae, 1928.

Seraphicae Legislationis Textus Originales, Ad Claras Aquas, 1897.

AUTHORS

Albertus a Bulsano, *Expositio Regulae Fratrum Minorum,* Oeniponte, 1850; Florentiae, 1864; Mediolani, 1889; Romae, 1932.

Alphonsus de Casarubios-Hieronymus a Sorbo, *Compendium Privilegiorum Fratrum Minorum,* 4. ed., Venetiis, 1609.

Angelus Clarenus, *Expositio Regulae Fratrum Minorum,* ed. L. Oliger, Ad Claras Aquas, 1912.

Anonymous, *Casus Regulae in Parisiensi, Tolosana, et Hollando-Belgica Ordinis FF. Min. S. Franc. Capuccinorum Provinciis Anno 1874 Propositi et Resoluti,* Tornaci, 1877.

Anonymous, *Doctrina para Criar los Novicios de la Orden de Nuestro Padre San Francisco,* Valladolid, 1718.

Anonymous, *Esposizione della Regola de' Frati Minori di S. Francesco,* Firenze, 1594.

Anonymous, *Quaestiones Quaedam de Ieiunio et Abstinentia in Ordine Fratrum Minorum,* Romae: Apud Curiam Generalem Ordinis Fratrum Minorum Capuccinorum, 1942.

Antonio da Patti, *Considerationi et Espositioni sopra Tutti li Precetti della Regola de' Frati Minori del Serafico P. S. Francesco,* Venetia, 1615.

Antonius M. de Corduba, *Expositio Evangelicae Regulae Seraphici Patris Sancti Francisci,* Venetiis, 1610.

Bartholomaeus de Pisa, "De Conformitate Vitae Beati Francisci ad Vitam Domini Iesu," *Analecta Franciscana,* Vol. V, Ad Claras Aquas, 1906.

Bartolucci, Silvester, *Minorica Fratrum Conventualium Sancti Francisci,* Perusiae, 1615.

Benoffi, Francescantonio, *Spirito della Regola de' Frati Minori,* Roma, 1807.

Bernardino da Siena, *Esposizione della Regola Francescana,* Firenze: Curia Provincializia dei Frati Minori Cappuccini, 1950.

Bernardinus von Gend, *Ausslegung ueber die Regel der Minderbrueder,* Coellen, 1721.

Bernardo da Bologna, *Lezioni sopra la Regola dei Frati Minori di S. Francesco,* Venezia, 1753.

Beste, Udalricus, *Introductio in Codicem,* editio altera, Collegeville, Minn.: Saint John's Abbey, 1944.

Bona-Gratia Habsensis, *Compendiosa Summula Selectarum Quaestionum Regularium,* Lugduni, 1671.

Bonaventura, S., *Legenda Maior S. Francisci Assisiensis et Eiusdem Legenda Minor,* Ad Claras Aquas; ex Typographia Collegii S. Bonaventurae, 1941.

——— *Opera Omnia,* Ad Claras Aquas, 1898, VIII.

Bonifatius a Ceva, *Speculum Minorum seu Firmamentum Trium Ordinum,* Venetiis, 1513.

Bouscaren, T. Lincoln, *The Canon Law Digest,* 3 vols., Milwaukee: Bruce, 1934–1954.

Bouscaren, T. Lincoln-O'Connor, James, *The Canon Law Digest* Annual Supplement through 1953, Milwaukee: Bruce, 1954; Annual Supplement through 1954, Milwaukee: Bruce, 1955; Annual Supplement through 1955, Milwaukee: Bruce, 1956.

Capobianco, Pacificus, *Privilegia et Facultates Ordinis Fratrum Minorum,* editio altera, Salerni, ex Conventu S. M. Angelorum, 1948.

Chassaing, Bruno, *Sanctus Franciscus Redivivus Regulae Minorum quam Christo Dictante Condiderat, Interpres,* Parisiis, 1652.

Christianus von Bienzheim, *Kurze Unterweisungen ueber die Regel der Minder-Brueder des heiligen Vaters Francisci,* Strasburgi, 1781.

Chronica Fratris Jordani, ed. H. Boehmer, Parisiis, 1908.

Chronologia Historico-Legalis Seraphici Ordinis, Vol. I, Neapoli, 1650; Vol. II, Venetiis, 1718; Vols. III–IV, Romae, 1752–1795.

Conte a Coronata, Matthaeus, *Institutiones Iuris Canonici,* 5 vols., Vols. I–II, 4. ed.; Vols. III–V, 3. ed., Romae: Marietti, 1947–1951.

Crousers, Cyprianus, *Lectiones Paraeneticae ad Regulam Seraphici Patris S. Francisci,* Coloniae Agrippinae, 1625.

Cuthbert, *Life of St. Francis of Assisi,* New York, 1921.

De Carlo, Camillus, *Jus Religiosorum,* Romae: Desclée, 1950.

De Gubernatis, Dominicus, *Orbis Seraphicus,* 6 vols., Vols. I–V, Romae, 1682–1689; Vol. VI, Ad Claras Aquas, 1886.

Deodatus a Bivona, *Esposizione Scolastica della Regola dei Frati Minori,* Palermo: Tip. "Fiamma Serafica," 1938.

Dernoye, Bonaventura, *Medulla S. Evangelii per Christum Dictata S. Francisco in sua Seraphica Regula Exposita Moraliter,* Coloniae Agrippinae, 1734.

Dionigi da Rossiglione, *La Regola del Serafico P. S. Francesco,* Alessandria, 1934.

Eduardus Alenconiensis, *Primigeniae Legislationis Ordinis Fratrum Minorum Capuccinorum Textus Originales,* Romae, 1928.

Engelbert Maria von Scheyern, *Geistliche Schule zur Unterweisung im Seraph. Leben,* Altoetting, 1906.

Eubel, Conradus, *Bullarii Franciscani Epitome sive Summa Bullarum in Eiusdem Bullarii Quattuor Prioribus Tomis Relatarum, Addito Supplemento,* Apud Claras Aquas, 1908.

Eugenio da Pontremoli, *Breve Esposizione della Regola Minoritana,* Firenze, 1911.

Expositio Quattuor Magistrorum super Regulam Fr. Minorum (1241–1242), ed. L. Oliger, Romae: Edizioni di "Storia e Letteratura," 1950.

Fanfani, Ludovicus, *De Iure Religiosorum,* 3. ed., Rhodigii: Instituto Paduano di Arti Grafiche, 1949.

Felder, Hilarin, *The Ideals of St. Francis of Assisi,* tr. Berchmans Bittle, New York, 1925.

Ferraris, Lucius, *Prompta Bibliotheca Canonica, Iuridica, Moralis Theologica, Ascetica, Polemica, Rubristica, Historica,* 8 vols., Romae, 1885–1889. Vol. nonum addidit Ianuarius Bucceroni, Romae, 1899.

Ferreres, Ioannes Baptista, *Compendium Theologiae Moralis,* 12. ed., 2 vols., Barcinone, 1923.

Fidel de Pamplona, *Ayunos de los Religiosos despuês de la Promulgación del Código,* Madrid: Instituto San Raimundo de Peñafort, 1953.

Filippo di Castellucio, *Dichiarazione Letterale, e Morale de' Precetti che si Contengono nella Regola de' Frati Minori di San Francesco,* Bologna, 1759.

Flaminio Annibali da Latera, *Manuale de' Frati Minori,* Roma, 1776.

Franciscus Assisiensis, S., *Opuscula,* Ad Claras Aquas: ex Typographia Collegii S. Bonaventurae, 1949.

Gabriel-Angelo da Vicenza, *La Regola de Frati Minori Esposta praticamente,* Venezia, 1758.

Gabriel-Angelo da Vicenza, *La Regola dei Frati Minori Esposta practicamente,* ed. Cosmas Sartori, 6. ed., Vicenza: Commisariato Terz' Ordine Francescano, 1937.

Gaetano Mari da Bergamo, *Istruzioni Morali, Ascetiche, sopra la Poverta de' Frati Minori Cappuccini di S. Francesco,* Padova, 1750.

Gaudenzio da Brescia, *Lo Spirito della Serafica Regola,* Brescia, 1761.

Georges de Villefranche, *Exposition de la Règle des Frères Mineurs,* Toulouse, 1893.

Giovanni Battista da Monza, *Espiacatione della Regola di San Francesco,* Napoli, 1647.

Goyeneche, S., *Quaestiones Canonicae de Iure Religiosorum,* 2 vols., Neapoli: M. d' Auria, Pontificius Editor, 1954–1955.

Gurney-Salter, Emma, *The Coming of the Friars to England & Germany, Being the Chronicles of Brother Thomas of Eccleston and Brother Jordan of Giano,* London, 1926.

Herrera, Antonio Parra, *Legislación Eclesiástica sobre el Ayuno y la Abstinencia,* The Catholic University of America, Canon Law Studies, n. 92, Washington: The Catholic University of America Press, 1935.

Hervé, J. M., *Manuale Theologiae Dogmaticae,* 4 vols., Parisiis: Apud Berche et Pagis, Editores, 1949–1951.

Hess, Beda M., *Manuale de Regula et Constitutionibus Ordinis Fratrum Minorum Conventualium,* Romae: Typis Polyglottis Vaticanis, 1942.

Hieronymus a Politio, *Expositio cum Dubiis Excussis in Regulam Seraphici Patriarchae S. Francisci,* Neapoli, 1606.

Holzapfel, Heribertus, *Manuale Historiae Ordinis Fratrum Minorum,* Latine redditum a Gallo Haselbeck, Friburgii Brisgoviae, 1909.

Huber, Raphael, *A Documented History of the Franciscan Order,* Milwaukee: Nowiny, 1944.

Hurter, Hugo, *Nomenclator Literarius Theologiae Catholicae,* 3. ed., 5 vols., Oeniponte, 1903–1913.

Jone, Heribertus, *Commentarium in Codicem Iuris Canonici,* 3 vols., Paderborn: Ferdinandus Schoeningh, 1950–1955.

Kazenberger, Kilianus, *Liber Vitae,* Oeniponte, 1761; nova editio, Assisi, 1899.

Kazenberger, Kilianus-Iglesias, Antonius, *Liber Vitae,* Ad Claras Aquas, 1926; editiones subsequentes, Romae: Pontificium Athenaeum Antonianum, 1948; 1954.

Kerckhove, Gaudentius, *Commentarii in Generalia Statuta Ordinis S. Francisci Fratrum Minorum Provinciis Germano-Belgicae,* Coloniae Agrippinae, 1709.

The Little Flowers of St. Francis of Assisi, New York: Catholic Book Publishing Co., 1950.

Louis de Paris, *Exposition Literale de la Règle des FF. Mineurs,* Paris, 1623.

Luchi, Bonaventura, *Nuova Manuale o Sia Istruzione Practica sopra la Regola e Costituzioni dell' Ordine de' P.P. Minori Conventuali di San Francesco,* Venezia, 1758.

Maas, Agatho, *Kurze Auslegung der Regel des heiligen Vaters Franziskus v. Assis,* Innsbruck, 1873.

Majocchi, Samuele, *Esposizione Ascetico-Morale della Regola Minoritana,* Piacenza, 1856.

Manero, Petrus, *Expositio Regulae Fratrum Minorum,* Gandavi, 1664.

Marchant, Petrus, *Expositio Literalis in Regulam S. Francisci,* Antverpiae, 1631.

———, *Fundamenta Duodecim Ordinis Fratrum Minorum S. Francisci,* Bruxellis, 1657.

Marinus a Neukirchen, *Constitutionum Generalium Primi Ordinis Seraphici Series Chronologica,* Romae: Institutum Historicum Ord. Fr. Min. Capuccinorum, 1942.

———, *De Capitulo Generali in Primo Ordine Seraphico,* Romae: Institutum Historicum Ord. Fr. Min. Capuccinorum, 1952.

Matthaeucci, Agostinus, *Schola Paupertatis,* Romae, 1731.

Merkelbach, Benedictus, *Summa Theologiae Moralis,* 8. ed., 3 vols., Parisiis: Desclée, 1949.

Michiels, Gommarus, *Normae Generales Juris Canonici,* editio altera, 2 vols., Romae: Desclée, 1949.

Mocchegiani, Petrus, *Iurisprudentia Ecclesiastica,* 3 vols., Ad Claras Aquas, 1904–1905.

Mondello, Paulo, *Espositione sopra li XXVII Precetti della Regola di S. Francesco,* Napoli, 1608.

Nicholas of Cork, *Fast and Abstinence in Franciscan Legislation,* Rome: Pontificia Universitas Gregoriana, 1943.

Piatus Montensis, *Praelectiones Iuris Regularis,* 3 vols., Vols. I–II, editio altera, Tornaci, 1888–1900.

———, *Pium Minoritae Vade-Mecum,* ed. ab Adolpho a Denderwindeke, Mechliniae, 1907.

Quaglia, Armando, *L'Originalità della Regola Francescana,* Sassoferrato: Scuola Tipographica Francescana, 1943.

Rapinaeus, Carolus, *Regula FF. Minorum Eiusque Spiritualis Expositio,* Chracas, 1711.

Regatillo, Eduardus, *Institutiones Iuris Canonici,* 4. ed., 2 vols., Santànderii: Sal Terrae, 1951.

Ricardo de Lizaso, *Exposición de la Regla de los Frailes Menores, Compendio de la Novísima Edición (1932) de la Obra del Mismo Título del P. Alberto de Bolzano,* Pamplona: PP. Capuchinos, 1939.—cited in the text as *Lizaso-Bolzano.*

Rodericus, Emanuel, *Quaestiones Regulares et Canonicae,* 2 vols., Venetiis, 1611.

Sanctes Thesaurus Romanus, *Expositio in Regulam Seraphici Patris S. Francisci, Quam in Latinam Transtulit Admodum V. P. F. Joducus, Bremgartensis Concionator,* Lucernae, 1675.

Sanctorus de Melfi, *Morales Commentarii in Statuta, & Constitutiones Ordinis Fratrum Minorum S. P. N. Francisci de Observantia,* Romae, 1643.

Santi Thesauro Romano, *Espositione sopra la Regola del Serafico Padre S. Francesco,* Roma, 1614.

Schaefer, Timotheus, *De Religiosis,* 4. ed., Romae: Typis Polyglottis Vaticanis, 1947.

Schmidt, John Rogg, *The Principles of Authentic Interpretation in Canon 17 of the Code of Canon Law,* The Catholic University of America, Canon Law Studies, n. 141, Washington: The Catholic University of America Press, 1941.

Seraphinus a Loiano, *Institutiones Theologiae Moralis,* 5 vols., Taurini: Marietti, 1934–1942.

Sleutjes, Michael, *Commentarius in Constitutiones Generales Fratrum Minorum,* Ad Claras Aquas, 1915.

Subaglio da Merato, Gieronimo Francesco, *Scola del Frate Minore,* Milano, 1654.

Thomas Aquinas, S., *Summa Theologica,* Taurini: Marietti, 1905.

Thomas de Celano, *Vita Prima S. Francisci Assisiensis,* Ad Claras Aquas, 1926.

———, *Vita Secunda S. Francisci Assisiensis* Ad Claras Aquas, 1927.

Trienekens, Isidorus, *Expositio Canonico-Moralis Regulae Fratrum Minorum,* 4. ed., Mechliniae: Typographia S. Francisci, 1948.

Ubach, I., *Compendium Theologiae Moralis,* 2 vols., Friburgii Brisgoviae, 1926–1927.

Valerio do Sacramento, *Thesouro Seraphico,* Coimbra, 1735.

Van Hove, Alphonsus, *De Privilegiis, De Dispensationibus,* Romae: Dessain, 1939.

Vermeersch, A.-Creusen, I., *Epitome Iuris Canonici,* 3 vols., Vols. I–II, 7. ed.; Vol. III, 6. ed., Romae: Dessain, 1946–1954.

Viatore da Coccaglio, *Tracce di Tradizione sopra la Regola de' Frati Minori,* Venezia, 1780.

Victorius ab Appeltern, *Compendium Praelectionum Iuris Regularis Adm. R. P. Piati Montani,* editio altera, Parisiis, 1913.

———, *Dissertatio de Modo Quo Diversa Ieiunia et Abstinentiae a Religiosis Familiis Hodiendum Sunt Observanda,* Romae, 1917.

Waddingus, Lucas, *Annales Minorum,* 3. ed., curavit Joseph Maria Fonseca, 27 vols., Ad Claras Aquas, 1931–1934.

Wernz, Franciscus, *Ius Decretalium,* 6 vols. in 10, Romae et Prati, 1898—1914.

Wernz, Franciscus-Vidal, Petrus, *Ius Canonicum,* 7 vols., Vols. I, VI, VII, 2. ed.; Vols. II, V, 3. ed., Romae: Apud Aedes Universitatis Gregorianae, 1933–1952.

Zeno von Ufering, *Erklaerung der Regel des heiligen seraphischen Vaters Franziskus,* Altoetting, 1929.

ARTICLES

Fidel de Pamplona, "Ayunos de los Religiosos después de la Promulgación del Código," *Revista Española de Derecho Canónico,* VIII (1953), 453–473.

———, "Ayunos y Abstinencias en la Regla Franciscana," *Ius Seraphicum,* I (1955), 268–294.

Ledwolorz, Adolphus, "De Superiorum potestate dispensandi in iure particulari Ordinis Fratrum Minorum," *Antonianum,* XIII (1938), 33–58.

Marinus a Neukirchen, "Constitutionum Generalium Primi Ordinis Seraphici Series Chronologica," *Collectanea Franciscana,* XII (1942), 377–396.

Robinson, Paschal, "Quo Anno Ordo Fratrum Minorum Inceperit" *Archivum Franciscanum Historicum,* II (1909), 181–186.

Victorius ab Appeltern, "De Modo quo diversa ieiunia et abstinentiae a religiosis Familiis hodiendum sunt observanda," *Ephimerides Liturgicae,* XXXI (1917), 56–63; 117–128; 181–192; 251–254; 396–400.

PERIODICALS

Antonianum, Romae, 1926—
Archivum Franciscanum Historicum, Ad Claras Aquas, 1908—
Collectanea Franciscana, Romae, 1931—
Ephimerides Liturgicae, Romae, 1881—
Franziskanische Studien, Muenster in W., 1914—; Werl in W., 1936—
Ius Seraphicum, Romae, 1955—
Miscellanea Franciscana, Romae, 1901—

ALPHABETICAL INDICES

I. Index of Names

II. Index of Subjects

BIOGRAPHICAL NOTE

Jordan Joseph Sullivan was born in Yonkers, New York, on July 13, 1922. He attended the schools of that city, graduating from Gorton High School in 1940. Thereupon he enrolled in Manhattan College, New York City, where he studied for two years. In 1942 he entered the novitiate of the Capuchin Order at Saint Felix Friary, Huntington, Indiana. After making profession in September, 1943, he continued his studies in philosophy at Mary Immaculate Friary, Garrison, New York, where he was awarded the degree of Bachelor of Arts in June, 1946. He pursued his study of theology at Saint Anthony Friary, Marathon, Wisconsin. On June 3, 1949, he was ordained to the priesthood in Saint Mary's Church, Marathon. His first assignment was to teach in Glenclyffe High School, the Capuchin minor seminary in Garrison, New York. In the fall of 1953 he began the study of Canon Law in the Gregorian University, Rome, Italy, receiving the degree of Bachelor of Canon Law in June of 1954, and the degree of Licentiate in Canon Law in June of 1955. In September, 1955, he enrolled in the School of Canon Law at the Catholic University of America.

CANON LAW STUDIES *

368. Bockstie, Rev. Richard, C.Ss.R., J.C.L., The principal oratory of religious.
369. Grajewski, Rev. Maurice J., O.F.M., M.A., Ph.D., J.C.L., The supreme moderator of exempt religious orders.
370. Havlik, Rev. Bernard J., A.B., J.C.L., The cessation of rescripts.
371. Olkovikas, Rev. Albert William, S.T.L., J.C.L., The *instantia* of the lawsuit.
372. Poblete, Rev. Elias Olarte, J.C.L., The plenary council.
373. Sokolich, Rev. Alexander F., S.T.L., J.C.L., Canonical provisions for universities and colleges.
374. Sullivan, Rev. Jordan J., O.F.M.Cap., B.A., J.C.L., Fast and abstinence in the First Order of St. Francis.
375. Kennedy, Rev. David W., J.C.L., Canon Law and liturgical music.

www.ingramcontent.com/pod-product-compliance
Lightning Source LLC
LaVergne TN
LVHW050213080826
844660LV00012B/406

* 9 7 8 0 8 1 3 2 2 5 3 6 4 *